The Book of
HORS D'OEUVRES AND CANAPES

The Book of
HORS D'OEUVRES
AND CANAPES

ARNO SCHMIDT
AND
INJA NAM

PHOTOGRAPHY BY
J.GERARD SMITH

VAN NOSTRAND REINHOLD
I(T)P® A Division of International Thomson Publishing Inc.

New York • Albany • Bonn • Boston • Detroit • London • Madrid • Melbourne
Mexico City • Paris • San Francisco • Singapore • Tokyo • Toronto

I(T)P® Van Nostrand Reinhold is a division of International Thomson Publishing, Inc.
The ITP logo is a registered trademark under license

Printed in the United States of America

For more information, contact:

Van Nostrand Reinhold
115 Fifth Avenue
New York, NY 10003

Chapman & Hall GmbH
Pappelallee 3
69469 Weinheim
Germany

Chapman & Hall
2-6 Boundary Row
London
SE1 8HN
United Kingdom

International Thomson Publishing Asia
221 Henderson Road #05-10
Henderson Building
Singapore 0315

Thomas Nelson Australia
102 Dodds Street
South Melbourne, 3205
Victoria, Australia

International Thomson Publishing Japan
Hirakawacho Kyowa Building, 3F
2-2-1 Hirakawacho
Chiyoda-ku, 102 Tokyo
Japan

Nelson Canada
1120 Birchmount Road
Scarborough, Ontario
Canada M1K 5G4

International Thomson Editores
Seneca 53
Col. Polanco
11560 Mexico D.F. Mexico

3   4   5   6   7   8   9   10   QEB-HK   01   00   99   98   97

Library of Congress Cataloging-in-Publication Data
Schmidt, Arno, 1937-
    The book of hors d'oeuvres and canapes / Arno Schmidt and Inja Nam;
photography by J. Gerard Smith.
        p.   cm.
    Includes index.
    ISBN 0-442-02045-7
    1. Appetizers.   I. Nam, Inja, 1935-   . II. Title.
TX740.S3234   1996
641.8'12—dc20

96-14907
CIP

http://www.vnr.com
product discounts • free email newsletters
software demos • online resources
email: info@vnr.com A service of I(T)P®

CONTENTS

CHAPTER 1

INTRODUCTION   1

CHAPTER 2

SELLING   5

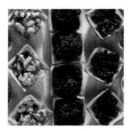

CHAPTER 3

SERVICE STYLES, SERVICE ISSUES, PRODUCTION POINTERS, AND LOGISTICS   11

RECIPE TABLE OF CONTENTS

BASIC RECIPES

COLD CANAPES

HOT HORS D'OEUVRES

How the Recipes are Organized

We chose to organize the recipes in groups, like wine lists, with clearly identifiable prefixes. This method should make it easy for you to find a recipe. The Recipe Table of Contents lists the recipes in chronological order within each group. When a recipe is needed as an ingredient within a recipe, it is always listed by recipe number and page.

CHAPTER 4
Basic Recipes

- **HT** (**H**ow **T**o) Recipes with illustrated preperation steps, start with #HT 100 and go to #HT 106.

- **RC** (**R**ecipes **C**anapes) Recipes for canapes start with #RC 50 and go to #RC 58.

- **R** (**R**ecipes for Hors d'Oeuvres) start with #R 106 and go to #R 179. They are classified as:

  - Batters, Dough, and other basic starch items: #R 106 to #R 128
  - Fillings for baked or steamed items #R 129 to #R165.
  - Dips, Marinades, Relishes, Sauces, and Miscellaneous start with #R 166 and go to #R 179.

CHAPTER 5
Cold Canapes

- The canape displays are organized alphabetically by themes and start with #C 101 and go to #C 124.

- Individual plated canapes start with #C 125 and go to #C154.

HOT HORS D'OEUVRES

- This large chapter contains a wide selection of hot hors d'oeuvres. In some cases, components described in Chapter 4, the recipes starting with the letter R, are used, in other cases the recipes are unique. Every time a component is used, the recipe and page number is given. All recipes in this chapter start with H (Hot).

- Baked Hors d'Oeuvres start with #H 101. Many of these items can be made ahead of time and baked or warmed in an oven. Most items are suitable for off-premise catering, and many items can be passed on trays (butler style).

- Barbecued, Broiled, and Grilled Hors d'Oeuvres start with #H 221. These items need a broiler or grill, and in most cases must be finished at the last moment. Some items would be difficult to produce off-premise.

- Fried Hors d'Oeuvres start with #H 243. A deep fat fryer is needed to make these items, which precludes their use in off-premise catering.

- International Hors d'Oeuvres start with #H 266, Oriental; #H 275, South of the Border; and #H 284, India.

- Pan- and Griddle-Fried Hors d'Oeuvres start at #H 291. Many of these items can be made off-premise.

- Roasted Hors d'Oeuvres start with #H 323. Many items can be pre-prepared, and finished at the last moment.

- Spoon Hors d'Oeuvres start with #H 333.

- Steamed Hors d'Oeuvres start with #H 339. Many items can be steamed at the last moment, and can be prepared off-premise.

ACKNOWLEDGMENTS

It takes the effort and cooperation of many people to write a book. My thanks go to my co-author, Inja Nam. She created the stunning canape displays, and made her patient husband chauffeur her to many shopping trips and to the photo studio.

I worked with Inja Nam at The Waldorf-Astoria Hotel where she is Chef Decorator. After we published *The Art of Garnishing* (VNR 1993), Inja started to talk about writing this book. We were encouraged by Melissa Rosati, Publisher at VNR, and after much planning, the book started to take shape.

We were fortunate that VNR hired again James Gerard Smith as photographer. He has unending patience, and is a font for ever new and exciting artistic ideas about presenting food.

There are many colleagues from whom I have learned during my 50 year career in the food service industry, but I would like to give special mention to friends who have directly contributed ideas and recipes to this book. They are: Rosemarie Aldin, Food Writer; Abigail Kirsch Culinary Productions; and Michel Teulet, Executive Chef.

Casa DiLisio Products, Mt. Kisco, New York, provided Pesto Sauce, and Fink Baking Company, Long Island City, New York, provided Sandwich Bread Sliced Lengthwise.

My thanks also go to the production staff and editors at VNR, who trimmed the text of this book to a manageable format and made it look beautiful.

Special thanks go to my wife Margaret. She became a computer widow again and had to spend many evenings and weekends without her husband because he was holed up in his office. In addition, she had to put up with many photo sessions in our New Jersey home, where the hors d'oeuvres pictures were taken. James Smith moved in a number of times with his equipment and props, and took over the dining room, kitchen, and sun room. The house became a film studio with all the excitement and inconveniences. Maragret managed to offer encouragement and advice. Thanks to her, and Jim's personality, we survived the sessions, and even continue to work on other projects.

The Book of
HORS D'OEUVRES
AND CANAPES

chapter 1

INTRODUCTION

The primary purpose of this book is to provide ideas and to stimulate the imagination when preparing canapes and hors d'oeuvres. The book also addresses production issues, service concerns, and logistical challenges.

The terms *canape* and *hors d'oeuvres* are foreign but have lost some of their original meaning. A *canapé* is a French word for *sofa* or *day bed*. The term was adapted by imaginative chefs for food that is put on something, normally a bread based support.

In today's vernacular the word *canape* has lost the accent mark, and is not necessarily the food items served on a piece of bread, toast, cracker, or even a base at all. However, it is always served cold. Shrimp on ice are billed as canapes, just as are celery sticks and carrots. Even a cheese board is considered canapes.

Hors d'oeuvres is also a French term. Literally it means "before the main object or work." In culinary usage it means "appetizer," either hot or cold. On French menus an hors d'oeuvre is normally a plated appetizer, such as pasta, paté, hot or cold seafood, marinated vegetables, and related items. On Italian menus the same items are listed as antipasto. In the United States the term hors d'oeuvres refers to hot appetizers, and canapes include bite size cold appetizers. *Hors d'oeuvres* is spelled in plural form.

Canapes and hors d'oeuvres are reception food and there are no limits to the imagination of the caterer or chef when creating them, much like giving a painter a palette of colors and unlimited freedom. Talented persons can produce amazing results. In this book we show both stunning displays, especially of cold canapes, and also hors d'oeuvres that can be produced economically.

The challenge of inventing canapes and hors d'oeuvres provides caterers the freedom to conceive something completely new, and sell it. However, before an item is sold it must be tested, tasted, and made for a small amount of people to get their comments and to iron out production and service kinks.

For many clients the reception food is the most important part of the meal. A caterer who can build a reputation for providing exciting canapes and hors d'oeuvres has a distinct advantage over the competition.

Although understanding the meaning of hospitality is basic to the industry, the catering business, like any other, must be profitable to stay in business, to reward the caterer for hard work, and to create the funds to improve the business.

Beside stimulating the imagination of the readers, this book will address the tricks of the trade and how to maximize profit without jeopardizing quality. Some canape displays in this book are stunningly beautiful, but by analyzing the photographs it becomes apparent that the beauty is based more on skillful display and imagination than on difficult production processes.

Canapes and hors d'oeuvres can be purchased ready to use. These are available in many quality levels and some caterers offer purchased items along with items made on premise. Customers often recognize canapes and hors d'oeuvres that were purchased and resent paying for products which have not been made in house.

Preparing canapes and hors d'oeuvres is labor intensive. In most cases the material cost is lower than the production labor cost. Many caterers prepare hors d'oeuvres or components of dishes, such as dough and fillings, ahead of time during slow periods and keep the items chilled or frozen until needed. Most dough and many fillings can be made ahead without any noticeable deterioration of quality.

The distinction between "from scratch" cooking and use of food ingredients in different stages of preparation, also called "convenience" foods, has been blurred. The food industry offers a wide variety of wonderful products and the skillful operator will use them to save labor and to achieve consistency. This book takes into consideration the many excellent products available on the market which provide significant labor savings without compromising quality.

Labor cost can vary greatly between particular hors d'oeuvres. This must be taken into consideration when menus are discussed with clients and proposals are prepared. Many salespersons do not know the labor needed to make each kind of canape and hors d'oeuvres. At best, they are aware of the cost of the raw materials. A well thought out proposal will skillfully combine high labor cost pieces with items that can be mass produced.

It is difficult to prorate other business expenses to each function. Large swings in business are inherent to the catering business. After business cycles have been identified, it is prudent to establish a percentage cost allocation which must be applied to each party. These costs include labor, office expenses, amortization or rent of the facility, and equipment, utilities, advertising, insurance, and profit. Rental fees for equipment are normally passed on to the customer with a handling fee of 10 percent over cost.

SELLING

Serving Hors d'Oeuvres and Canapes

Selling the right products

Canapes and hors d'oeuvres are served at just about all parties.

The primary function of parties is to bring people together. Offering guests food and drink as a token of hospitality when they arrive is deeply rooted in history. The caterer must be aware that food and drink are integral parts of a gathering, but in most cases must play a subordinate role and should not try to upstage the party.

When people are invited to a party it is unlikely that all will arrive at the same time. This premeal time window provides an opportunity to socialize. While the customers gather and wait for the main event, canapes, hors d'oeuvres, and beverages are served to break the ice and pass the waiting time. Food choices can be as simple as pretzels or as elaborate as luxurious canapes and hors d'oeuvres passed by servers or those served from buffets. Often a meal follows the reception.

On some occasions refreshments are not followed by a meal. Such events could include the inauguration of a gallery, a speech, a seminar, or a religious event, among others. It is expected that some refreshments will be served, but the customers will have dinner elsewhere. The food offered can consist of simple cookies, snacks, or canapes and hors d'oeuvres.

In some cases the reception is the meal, and Abigail Kirsch, a very successful caterer in Tarrytown, New York, has coined the phrase: "Dinner by the bite." At these events the food is so plentiful that it substitutes for a meal.

Matching Food and Service to the Occasion

The food is expected to be delicious, eye catching, elegant, exciting, and plentiful. Yet it should never detract from the main reason for the gathering, which in most cases is conversation and the opportunity to socialize.

The caterer must keep the purpose of the event in focus. Food can be elegant or informal. The timing of service is important, especially when speeches are scheduled. Food that takes too long to eat, or distracts from the purpose of the event, is not appropriate.

Taste must be a major consideration. A frequent comment at parties is that the food looks nice, but has no taste. Taste depends on the raw material used, the care and timing in preparation, and how it is handled. As a general rule food should be well flavored, because it is consumed in small bites and accompanied by drinks. However, nobody likes surprises and party food should never be so highly seasoned that customers gasp after eating a bite. As an example, fried chilies and other hot foods would not be welcome by unsuspecting customers. The main component of a dish should also be recognizable when possible.

If the event is given to honor someone, the caterer should try to find out the food preferences of the guest of honor. In some cases, this food would not be appropriate to serve to all others attending the party, but a special dish could be provided for the guest of honor.

When canapes and hors d'oeuvres are selected a number of factors should be taken into consideration. The overriding concerns are the customer's wishes, expectations, and budget, *but* the caterer must also take logistics into account. A party has "to work" smoothly and efficiently and if it does not run as expected, for whatever reason, the caterer will be blamed, the party giver embarrassed, and the caterer's reputation damaged.

Most customers are wise enough to listen to the advice of the caterer, providing the caterer has established a relationship based on a genuine desire to listen, to please, and to make the customer's ideas happen. If the caterer feels strongly that types of food, beverage, or service formats do not work well, the customer should be strongly advised not to insist on it. When a customer is not willing to compromise it is best for the caterer to refuse to handle the party rather than risk ruining his or her reputation.

The time of day and length of the party are a major consideration when matching food and service to the party. On premise caterers are basically in the real estate business and are concerned about when the function room will become available again. Most parties are limited to four hours, which also corresponds to music contracts and server shifts. Any time over four hours is considered overtime and might incur additional charges.

Off premise caterers rent most equipment and the rental expense is tied to the time used. Caterers schedule functions carefully and on busy days have staff working two parties.

Assessing the Customer's Profile

The caterer must find the common denominator that will meet most customer expectations. Food that is very personal, avant garde, or exotic will not be appreciated. The level of expectations changes by income, geography, season, and education levels. All people have pronounced likes and dislikes of food. Meals considered excellent by one group can be poorly rated by others.

The caterer should try to find out as much as possible about the demographics and expectations of the invited guests, as well as the age, ethnic background, economic levels, and other pertinent information about the customers. The taste of the party giver does not always accurately reflect the taste of those invited, who also have to be pleased. Food on the cutting edge of gastronomy might not appeal to many people.

There are also ethnic, religious, and nutritional issues to consider. For example, vegetarian and low calorie choices should be available at all parties.

Estimating Food Quantities

The length of the party plays a part in determining food quantities. When the reception lasts about one and one-half hours and is followed by a dinner, four pieces of hors d'oeuvres and three canapes are calculated for each customer.

When the reception is early, right after office hours, people are hungry, and about 10 to 12 pieces of canapes and hors d'oeuvres are needed per person. These receptions are expected to last until dinner time at 7:30 or 8:00 P.M.

When the reception starts at about 6 P.M. and is not followed by dinner, much more food is needed. A minimum of 12 to 14 canapes and hors d'oeuvres pieces per person are needed. Buffets with more substantial food should be encouraged for these parties.

Weddings normally have an extended social hour and at least 12 to 14 pieces per person should be calculated. The caterer should inquire how many children will attend and be sure to provide suitable food for them.

When the service is butler style, the flow of food can be regulated by the caterer. When the budget is tight, butler-style service is preferred, because the customers do not know how much food is actually served. Buffets can be eaten clean in a short time and when not replenished, it indicates to all customers that there was not enough food.

One common problem in the industry is accurately estimating quantities. As a result, caterers either run out of food too early into the party, or have food left over. The caterer must monitor the food consumption if possible and always have some reserve available for unexpected demand. How much people actually eat is very difficult to estimate with any degree of accuracy.

Ease of Preparation Considerations

The complexity of food preparation should not discourage the caterer from selling to the customer the canapes and hors d'oeuvres desired *providing* the price covers all costs and profit needs. There is a great difference in labor cost between types of canapes and hors d'oeuvres. It is obvious that items which can be produced efficiently and have a comparable food cost should be promoted over items with high labor cost.

There are many hors d'oeuvres listed in this book which can be made efficiently in large quantities. For example, flavored biscuits, silver dollars, cream puff items, and fritters in many varieties are less labor intensive than steamed food wrapped in rice wafer paper or filo bundles.

It is prudent for the person in charge of food production to meet frequently with the sales personnel to discuss production issues. These meetings should also be an exchange of ideas between the sales staff and the production staff. The sales staff is in contact with the customers and can provide important suggestions about culinary trends and expectations.

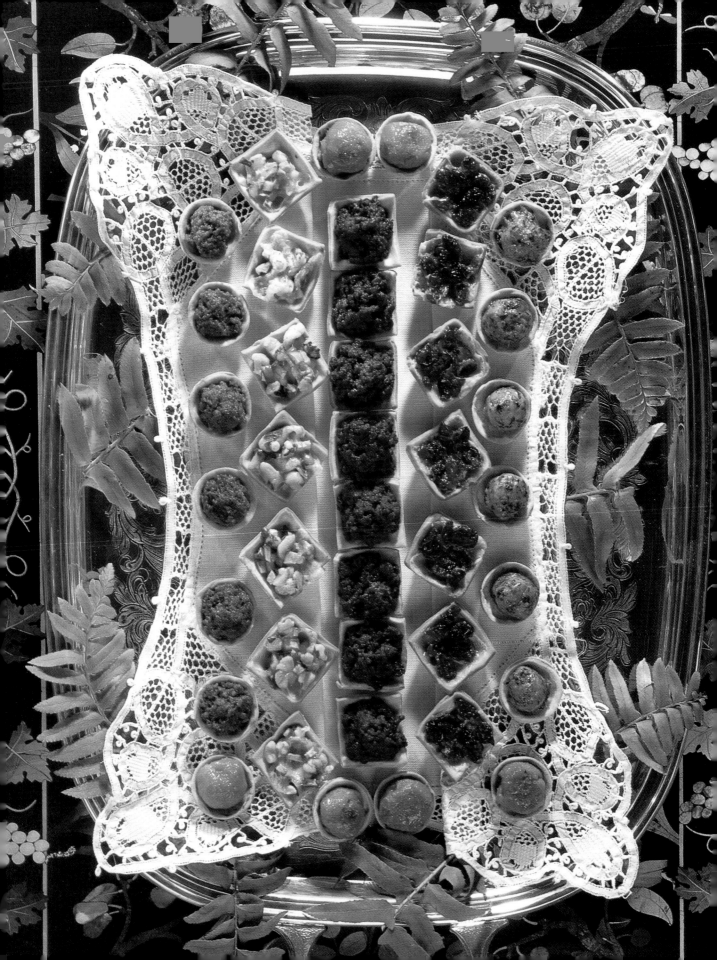

chapter

SERVICE STYLES, SERVICE ISSUES, PRODUCTION POINTERS, AND LOGISTICS

Service Styles

When selling a party, the type of service selected is a major consideration because it has an impact on food, labor cost, time, and space.

There are two ways of serving canapes and hors d'oeuvres—either passed by servers, called "butler style," or from buffets. In some cases a combination of both is used. Each service style has distinct features and advantages.

The type of service is important because it governs the food choices. Finger foods are suitable for butler service because the items can be picked up and eaten without utensils. In these cases, canapes and hors d'oeuvres should never be larger than bite size.

Butler style is used when a relatively small quantity of food is served, when all canapes and hors d'oeuvres are finger food, and when there is enough space for servers to circulate with platters.

Most hors d'oeuvres that are prepared with sauces require plates and forks and are best served from buffets. Even when served from buffets, food should be bite size. It is difficult to eat while standing up and holding a beverage.

When space in the banquet room is restricted or the kitchen is far, butler style service is difficult. Servers are not able to maneuver through the crowds with trays of food. The unhappy result is that some customers may not get much food or drink. Sometimes it happens that there may be ample food left over in the kitchen, because servers were not able to serve it. The customers leave with the impression that not enough food was available. In such cases it might be advisable to provide numerous minibuffets on small tables, sideboards, or even window sills. Safety is obviously a concern and no chafing dishes should be placed in spaces where they could be hazardous.

Buffets, also called stations, require circulation space and more equipment than butler style service, which requires platters, but they offer an opportunity to provide a larger selection of food. The distinction between appetizer buffets consisting of canapes and hors d'oeuvres and dinner buffets is not well defined. On some occasions, especially weddings, the buffets can be rather elaborate and contain pasta, carving stations, and other substantial food.

Behind the kitchen door

Butler style service food pointers

Hors d'oeuvres should conform to the following guidelines:

• Look fresh and appetizing.

• Not be soggy.

• Not be smelly; bad breath is very offensive.

• Be recognizable within reason. Many people have strong likes and dislikes for food and some have allergies. It is awkward to ask servers about ingredients, because in many cases the servers might not know the answer. Chances are the servers work as extras who have not been briefed about the party food.

• Not be filling except when the event is *not* followed by a dinner.

• Be dietarily correct. The hors d'oeuvres selection should always include vegetarian choices and items without pork and shellfish. There is a large and growing segment of people who adhere to a selective diet for personal or religious reasons.

• Be nutritionally correct. Customers generally are less concerned about diets during receptions than during sit-down meals, but some shun "fattening" dishes.

• Be interesting and fun. Canapes can be a little whimsical, can offer little surprises, and in some instances may help to keep the conversation going.

• Contain no bad surprises, such as very seasoned (hot) food or generally unacceptable ingredients when they are not recognizable.

• Meet the general expectations and eating habits of the customers. People have different taste levels and expectations.

• Not be boring.

• Food is there to be eaten. Nothing should be served unless it can be enjoyed with a minimum of fuss.

• Be easy to eat — toppings should not fall off. Even giving the impression that it could ruin a dress or suit will turn customers off.

• Be finger food, and little if anything should be left to pick up. Food should be the size that it can be popped right into the mouth. If two bites are needed, it is too big.

• Customers should not be standing with toothpicks or other inedible items to dispose of in flower vases or on the floor.

• Serving temperature should be sensible. Hot hors d'oeuvres should be served warm, not so hot that an unsuspecting person can get burned when eating one.

Butler-style service garnish pointers

• Hot food does not need much decoration; a variety of sizes, shapes, and types of platters provides the visual appeal.

• Elaborate garnishes which take away from the edible food should be avoided.

• The same hors d'oeuvres should not always be served on the same platters. As the platters are returned by the servers to the kitchen, they should be cleaned and refilled with the items that happen to be ready.

• The best decorations for hors d'oeuvres are the platters and other serving dishes themselves.

• Decorations should make sense and should not interfere with safety, speed of service, and convenience. Clumsy decorations can topple over or obstruct easy access to the food on the platter.

• It should be readily apparent that decorations are decorations—not meant to be eaten.

• Decorations should harmonize with the items served or with the theme of the party. Suitable decorations on hot hors d'oeuvres platters are live flowers or carved vegetable flowers fastened with bamboo skewers to a vegetable base. They should be kept cold or in ice water when not in use and must always look fresh, not wilted.

• Other appropriate decorations are small sculptures made of bread or salt dough or other food related items. Inedible pieces may include displays made with shellfish shells, or little baskets filled with a variety of the predominant ingredients for the dish. For instance, stuffed vegetables can be garnished with a display of tiny fresh vegetables. A platter with crayfish fritters can be garnished with a small nosegay of whole red crayfish.

• Decorations should be glued onto a hot platter with a paste made of flour and egg white diluted with water. The decoration will adhere immediately to the platter, but can be taken off when the servers return.

• Decorations must be out of the way to allow easy access to the food. The decorations should be at the far end of the platter, and the servers instructed to present the platters accordingly.

• Parsley is an herb that should not be sprinkled indiscriminately over all food leaving the kitchen. The same is true for little sprigs of herbs, which are not really edible and fall off the platter.

• When used properly, fresh herbs can make a quality statement. A small vase or container filled with a tiny bouquet of fresh herbs can make a very attractive decoration on the platter.

• Avoid sauces and dips. They are difficult to handle when the food is passed on platters.

• When sauces or dips are served, they should be in a shallow dish on the same platter with the food.

• Sauces and dips must be easily accessible and the quantity should correspond to the number of items on the platter. It is annoying when platters with hot food are still passed and the sauce is already depleted.

• Putting sauces into hollowed out fruits and vegetables should be done with caution and common sense. In most cases, the containers are not big enough to hold much sauce, and they can look messy in a short time. Also, if the vegetable is normally not eaten uncooked, it should not be used. For instance, putting a dip in a hollowed out acorn squash is not appetizing, because this squash is not eaten raw.

Butler style service, equipment pointers

• Off premise caterers should ask the customers whether they should use their own dishes. The danger that the dishes could be damaged should be pointed out. The serving pieces, such as trays, bowls, or platters must be small and compact.

• The serving platters should be light so the servers can carry them without getting tired.

• The dishes and service platters can consist of baskets, copper plates, china, silver, glass, and whimsical dishes providing they are safe, sanitary, and practical.

• Different size platters and serving dishes are useful to tailor the amount of food sent out as needed.

• Using platter of different shapes and sizes avoid monotony. Not every dish and platter must look the same.

• The service dishes must be scrupulously clean. Customers brush against them when servers maneuver in tight spaces. Cleanliness is elementary, but as dishes are refilled in the kitchen, occasionally continued cleanliness is overlooked.

• Beverage glasses should be easy to carry and to hold. Wine glasses with octagonal stems are easier to hold than glasses with round stems. Glasses should not be too tall. Big hurricane-shaped wine glasses are difficult to drink from.

Timing in butler style service

• Customers arrive at different times. Food service should be staggered so even late arrivals still get the full selection. This should be made clear to the kitchen personnel. Many cooks have the tendency to have all items ready at the beginning of the party.

• As the party goes on, a preference pattern will develop. Some items will be more popular than others. The caterer has an opportunity to decide which items to hold back and which to promote (push) so there is always a variety of items available to be passed.

• The platters should be filled depending on customers' response. When few people are present, the dishes should be less filled than when the room is crowded. This is when different sized platters are useful.

Buffet food and equipment pointers

• Food can be more elaborate and substantial than butler service because plates and forks are provided.

• The buffet table and the food itself can be decorated attractively.

• Buffets provide to the culinary staff an opportunity to display artistic talents, but it must be kept in mind that food should look edible, fresh, and appetizing.

• Centerpiece decorations on buffets should be tall.

They identify the location of the buffet table and provide a visual focal point. Centerpiece decorations should not be integrated with food, because when the food is gone, the decoration will remain on the table.

• Centerpieces can consist of natural flowers or flowers carved from vegetables, carved ice, old vases, silver pieces, candelabra, statues, or other suitable props. Some chefs pride themselves in making tallow or wax centerpieces; however, these are old fashioned, and unless the pieces are artistically attractive, should not be used.

• Centerpieces should not be meant to be eaten. If centerpieces are accessible to the customers and are edible, they will be picked over very quickly and look shabby for the rest of the event.

• Because of increased concern for nature and the ecology, animal trophies are no longer acceptable.

• Spotlights can enhance the food and decorations when placed strategically.

• Edible pieces should not touch displays not meant to be eaten.

• Food should look sanitary. Anything that looks handled and overworked is not appetizing.

• The attractiveness of buffets is very much dependent on the equipment. Beautiful china platters, silver chafing dishes, mirrors, and raisers add to the beauty.

• Chafing dishes come in many shapes and price ranges. It is important to have an ample amount of food pans (inserts) so food can be replenished easily.

• The size of platters should correspond with the amount of food displayed. Platters should be filled with as much food so they do not get depleted fast.

• Large display platters or mirrors are unattractive once empty, and are hard to remove. If large, attractive platters are available, they can be used as bases on which smaller bowls are placed. These smaller containers can be exchanged easily.

• Food should be in small portions. Anything that requires cutting with a knife does not belong on a canape and hors d'oeuvres buffet, since customers have no place to sit down.

- The plates the customers will use should not be larger than 5 in. (125 mm) in diameter (generally referred to as bread and butter plates).

- Forks should also be small — they are often called salad forks. Large forks have a tendency to slide off the plate. Knives should not be necessary.

- There can never be too many plates and forks. Customers like to come back for more food. At least three sets per customer should be available, some kept in reserve.

- As the party progresses, some of this equipment can be washed and recycled.

- Napkins should be plentiful, small, and not starched. Good quality paper napkins are better than large cloth dinner napkins.

- Hot food serving pieces should be user friendly. Serving tongs are often too big and awkward to use. There should be an ample supply of serving forks, spoons, and spatulas.

- Serving pieces should have long, insulated handles that do not slide into the hot chafing dishes.

- Precise timing information on the function (order) sheet is important. If the starting of the party is not clearly indicated, the buffet is either set up too early and gets stale, or is too late when the first customers arrive. Precise timing is an educated guess and the staff must be flexible.

- The estimated conclusion of the party should also be part of the function sheet, so the kitchen staff can time the flow of food accordingly.

- Making attractive hors d'oeuvres is a challenge. In most cases they are brown and are enhanced primarily by the platters, chafing dishes, and other table equipment from which they are served.

- Avoid superfluous decorations. Decorations on hot food are an integral part of a dish and are meant not only to embellish, but also to be eaten.

- Do not bury food under, or place on top of, items that will not be eaten.

Location and setup of buffets

- Off premise caterers should ask the customers to move or protect delicate furniture, objects d'art, and other items of importance that can be damaged.

- Many smaller buffets are better than one large buffet. They allow for easier movement and help to disperse the customers. Each buffet should have the same food, or should be clearly identified so customers know where they will find certain items.

- Location is crucial. Buffets should provide convenient access for customers and servers. They should not be close to high traffic areas, such as doors or corridors.

- Cafeteria-style lines should be avoided. Plates and flatware should be provided in several places, so there is no clear beginning of a line.

- Round buffets provide equal access, and food should be displayed in duplicate to avoid crowding.

- The buffets should be placed close to the kitchen if possible so they can be replenished without having the servers cross customer space.

- Buffets take up room, but well-placed buffets and bars disperse the crowd and draw them into spaces which would otherwise not be utilized.

- Never place buffets in front of fire exits or block fire exits with furniture or props.

- Space for customers to deposit soiled equipment should be plentiful. There can never be too many tables and counters for customers to drop off used equipment.

- Stand-up counters for eating are better than tables with chairs because they encourage mingling.

- Some chairs should be available for elderly people or for people who would like to sit down for a while. Chairs should not be placed against the wall and not around tables, to discourage customers from forming circles.

Service Issues

Server behavior

• Servers should always be attentive, and watch their customers unobtrusively. It is irritating when customers need something and servers do not notice.

• Servers should be courteous. People should be addressed formally at all times. Servers should always step back and let customers pass first through a door or hallway. If something is needed, servers should get it right away.

• Customers are always right. There is no deviation from this rule.

• Do not prejudge guests by appearance or ethnic background.

• Customers like efficient service. Servers should never act and look rushed or run in a dining room (or the back of the house for that matter), yet should be able to quickly produce what customers need.

• Servers should enjoy their work. Serving banquets can be hard work, but it is a rewarding occupation.

• Servers should be friendly; customers like to deal with human beings. However, servers should never get involved in lengthy, personal conversations.

• Customers like to be greeted. Servers should use common sense when greeting customers in a banquet situation, but when approaching a table the first time, a friendly greeting is appropriate.

• Servers should help customers and fellow workers as much as possible. Serving a banquet is a team effort in the kitchen and in the dining room.

• It is important for servers to learn how to listen.

• Servers should keep the hands out of sight, but not in pockets. They should never touch guests or coworkers and should keep one hand behind the back when not needed.

• Servers should never blame somebody for a mishap; no matter who is at fault, do not blame the kitchen, the caterer, or another worker if something goes wrong.

• Servers must be polite. Always, regardless of any provocation.

• Good posture is important. Servers should stand erect, and should not slouch, dance from one foot to the other, or lean on furniture.

• A genuine smile is the best way to demonstrate a positive attitude. Everyone looks better with a natural smile.

• Servers should show concern—little touches count. Every person is an individual with likes and dislikes, special dietary needs and, perhaps, handicaps.

• Servers should be swift. Nobody wants to wait. They should try to accomplish every task as quickly as possible without giving the impression of rushing.

- Servers should speak in good, plain English. If from another country, servers should not converse with fellow countrymen in their native language. Servers should never use slang. If a customer is not fluent in English and the server happens to speak the language well, he or she might offer to help.

- Servers should try to speak in terms of "we" and "us" when referring to other team members.

Server supervision, staffing levels, and policies

Part-time servers are hired for a particular job as "extra employees." Supervising servers in large, dispersed dining rooms or suites is difficult, and measuring the productivity of servers is hard to assess. Invariably some servers will work harder than others.

Constant, even handed, and fair supervision is needed at all times to provide the service the customers expect.

As the party progresses and the customers become more relaxed, servers also get more casual and get tired bussing soiled china, resupplying the buffet, serving food, or carrying out any other duties. The service level drops noticeably after the first hour at most parties. This is the time when supervision is needed most.

The number of servers needed for each function varies and is dependent on:

- Distance from the kitchen or pantry
- Amount of food to be served
- Expected quality level of service
- Size and configuration of banquet room
- The budget

General guidelines are:

- Butler style reception: One server for 50 customers.
- Buffet, assisted: One server for 40 customers.
- Buffet, self service: One server for 60 customers.
- Sit-down dinner, formal: One server for 10 customers.
- Sit-down dinner, informal: One servers for 20/25 customers.
- Open bar: One bartender for 60/80 customers.
- Cash bar: One bartender for 50/60 customers.

"Roll call" is a service meeting that should be held before every function by the caterer or banquet or dining room manager. The following points should be covered:

- The names of the host/hostess and special guests
- The purpose of the function
- The approximate length of the event
- The menu and service sequence
- Special concerns of the customers

- House policy of the caterer
- Questions from the servers

The "roll call" should always include a tour of parts of the premise that will be used for the party, including toilet rooms, loading areas or back door, and "off limit" sections, but not private quarters.

Suggested service policies

Accidents:

• Breakage: Equipment dropping happens at most parties. Broom and dustpan must be ready to sweep up debris.

• Spills: The banquet manager or manager must be alerted if the spill is on a customer. Plenty of clean, unstarched napkins should be ready and offered. If the spill is severe, but there are no injuries, the caterer might offer to get the garment dry cleaned.

• Injury/Illness: If there is an injury or illness, the customer should be asked if 911 should be called. Do not offer medical advice or treatment besides basic first aid. The host should be advised. Keep employees and guests discreetly away. Do not interrupt the party. Never dispense any medication of any sort, not even an aspirin.

• Floor spills: Secure the area right away to prevent customers or employees from slipping. This can be done by placing a chair over the spill or putting a towel over it. Decide beforehand who is responsible for cleanup, and be sure that a clean mop and bucket is available.

Suggested service policies concerning buffet maintenance

• Depleted platters must be removed and replaced. Plates, napkins, and flatware should always be plentiful.

• Platters and dishes should be easy to reach.

• When dishes are refilled, the food should be the same.

• The best way to refill platters is by exchange. This requires two servers.

• One server will bring the new supply, and another server will simultaneously remove the empty platter or insert.

• Under no circumstances should food be brought from the kitchen in bulk and dumped into containers or on platters.

• When empty platters are removed and not replaced, the remaining platters on the table should be rearranged if possible to cover the empty spot.

• Buffets should always look inviting and plentiful. It is obvious that buffets cannot be kept filled with food until the party is over.

• The manager will decide when to close down buffets. When there is more than one buffet, the food can be consolidated.

• The manager should consult with the kitchen staff when buffets are consolidated. The natural tendency of servers is to keep the buffet supplied at all times, regardless of cost.

• The caterer and kitchen staff prepare the food quantities required based on the order (function) sheet. If there is no good coordination between the dining room management and the kitchen, the flow of food is not regulated.

• When buffets are consolidated and shut down, the empty buffet table should still look attractive. It should be covered with clean linen if possible. Dirty tables look disgusting.

Suggested general service policies

• During butler style service all servers should carry cocktail napkins. In addition, napkins should be placed at strategic locations in the room. The servers should be instructed to offer napkins automatically. Some customers are distracted when taking an item and forget to take a napkin.

• Servers should not be allowed to nibble and drink alcoholic beverages. This is difficult to control. Servers should be provided by the caterer with a limitless supply of designated soft drinks. A meal should be provided *before* service. The cost of employee meals is the caterer's responsibility.

• Continuous collection of soiled equipment must be enforced. A server never goes empty handed into the back of the house. Equipment is collected on trays when practical. Servers should never put their fingers in empty soiled glasses.

• Tableware should be brought to the table on trays or platters, never in a fist. Exceptions are plates and fresh glasses.

• Smoking by guests has become a delicate issue. There should be tables without ashtrays available and designated with signs as smoke-free tables.

• Smoking by servers should not be allowed. Today, most customers are smoke sensitive and are repulsed by a server who just stole a smoke in a back corner. If a server must smoke—and many still do—encourage them to use a mouth spray to mask the odor.

• When wine is served at the table, it is always served before the food. The glasses should be filled when the food arrives.

Production

The keys to production efficiency are sufficient work space, tight scheduling of employees, ample refrigerated storage, and good equipment, including machinery.

Great swings in demand are inherent to the catering business. Peak periods are followed by slow stretches. Some caterers tell customers that everything is made fresh on premise from scratch. This is not always practical and truthful. The question can be raised: What was the starting point when these items were made from scratch?

Many caterers prepare food, or the components of dishes, ahead of time and chill or freeze them to use labor and equipment efficiently.

Equipment capability

Food production is governed by the availability and capacity of cooking equipment. Service style is dictated by the availability of service equipment. Although equipment can be rented, it is not always available when needed, or there is no space in which to use it efficiently.

On premise caterers have less equipment limitations because they have the time to maximize the use of cooking and refrigeration equipment. The equipment crunch is more often experienced in tabletop and buffet equipment when an operation has a number of banquet rooms and the same props are needed at the same time for different functions.

Holding concerns

Some hot food can be kept hot for a limited time without loosing too much quality. Cold food must also be handled properly when prepared ahead of time; some food keeps better than others. Hot food holding can be divided into dry holding and moist holding. Fried food and baked items generally should be kept in dry heat, the rest in moist heat.

It is still industry practice to keep food hot in heaters heated by canned fuel. The fuel gives off a strong odor, which eventually penetrates the food. Electric heaters in turn can develop a stale odor unless they are kept scrupulously clean.

Food specifications

Every time food is received, stored, handled, and processed it costs money. Food is available in many sizes, grades, and quality levels. The caterer must develop concise food specifications which detail exactly the size, shape, grade, and quality of each product that will be purchased. Although there will be occasional changes to accommodate customers' wishes, the basic specifications should not vary much. Based on these specifications, order sheets can be developed and prices can be checked between purveyors.

As an example, Parmesan cheese can be purchased from a number of countries; and in addition whole, or grated, or freshly grated, or dry. The caterer must decide on the quality and whether to grate the cheese on premise — providing the equipment is available — or purchase the cheese from a reputable purveyor.

The public awareness of organically grown fruits and vegetables, and organically raised meat is growing. A free " Green Cuisine Dictionary," listing sources is available to food service professionals by writing to Green Cuisine, Public Voice for Food and Health Policy, 1101 14th Street NW, Suite 710, Washington, DC 20005, (202) 371-1840.

Choosing between homemade and prepared products

The term *convenience food* is old fashioned and refers to products which can be used with little or no preparation. The key for using these products is customer acceptance. Most customers know when a product is purchased, when it looks machine made, and recognize it when it was served already someplace else.

The food service industry offers a large variety of semiprepared or fully prepared ingredients or components of dishes. Many of these products are of excellent quality and can save considerable time and labor cost if used properly. The list of ready-to-use products is long and is growing longer every day. The wise caterer will judiciously choose the products and methods which can save time and money without jeopardizing quality.

The quality of an item is judged by the customers by its freshness at the time of service. Consequently, all products should be baked, fried, or filled as close to service time as possible.

If the caterer employs a permanent staff, the employees must be kept busy when there is no business. To purchase items ready to use, and have the staff stand idle would not make much sense providing the employees have the skill to prepare the items efficiently.

The production schedule must be set up to make hors d'oeuvres and canape components ahead of time, and finish the canapes as close to the service period as possible. Cold canapes are labor intensive. They can seldom be made ahead of time and frozen.

Most hors d'oeuvres are made with dough which can be chilled or frozen before baking without losing quality. The exception is cream puff paste. Baked cream puffs, however, keep well for a few days.

Most fillings can be made ahead of time and chilled or frozen. Many hors d'oeuvres can be shaped and chilled for a few days. Cookies keep well and can be made during down time.

Ice carvings and other decorations can be homemade ahead of time or purchased. Ice sculptures will eventually dry out if left uncovered in a freezer for a long time.

Ready-made canapes do not freeze well. The bread gets soggy and in most cases the topping gets dry.

Purchased food components that are a great timesaver

• Puff paste dough. Few operations are equipped to make it efficiently because it requires expertise, a cool room, a large pastry table, and good refrigeration to store the dough. Much rolling is required which is best done with a machine. Frozen puff paste made with either butter or other fats is available and is ready to use. To make puff pastry on premise is in most cases not practical.

• Fresh vegetables in various stages of cleaning. This will reduce storage space and garbage. For example, fresh garlic is available peeled whole or chopped. Fresh onions are available peeled whole and sliced or diced. Many produce companies will clean and cut vegetables to specifications. This is important when refrigeration space is limited.

• Frozen chopped vegetables are perfectly adequate in many fillings. It is hard to tell the difference between fresh and frozen vegetables when the fillings are seasoned and baked.

• Completely trimmed meat. Meat can be purchased in many different trimming and boning phases. The caterer can order exactly the items needed without waste and preparation labor. Although this meat more expensive than meat purchased in primal cuts, it is still cheaper, unless the caterer has uses for the trimmings. Meat cutting requires skill and a sanitary environment, which is often not available. The same is true for fish; but it should be remembered that fish, once handled — cut in fillets — is more perishable than whole fish.

• Ground white meat turkey, readily available is perfectly acceptable when making poultry mousse. It is cheaper than chicken breast, and the caterer does not have to worry about contaminating the meat grinder with chicken.

• There are many acceptable biscuit, and muffin batter mixes on the market. They can be used when necessary. However, some have a high sugar content and are not suitable for hors d'oeuvres.

• Prepared pesto sauce. The supply, and the price, of fresh basil varies greatly during the year. Making pesto is also labor intensive because the leaves must be stripped from the stems.

• Shucked fresh clams.

• Raw shrimp, peeled and deveined for fried shrimp dishes.

• Unbaked hors d'oeuvres, not baked, freeze rather well, and there are some good products on the market. Many caterers keep a supply in stock and supplement their own products with purchased hors d'oeuvres when there is high demand.

Sanitation

The danger of food contamination and food poisoning is ever present. Caterers must observe the strictest sanitary safeguards to assure the customers of safe products.

• Food must be kept out of the danger temperature zone which is between 45°F/8°C and 140°F/60°C. Food thermometers should be used by all kitchen supervisors.

• Refrigeration should be rented when the refrigeration available is not adequate.

- Employees with open sores or infections should not be allowed to work.

- Food that will not be cooked, such as canapes, should be handled with gloves.

- Efficient garbage removal and recycling regulations must be observed.

- Small, single tank commercial dishwashers are a great timesaver and sterilizes small utensils, pots, and pans. Under-counter models take up no more space than a household size machine but operate on cycles under 5 minutes.

Logistical Challenges Which Are the Same for Both Types of Caterers

- Good communication and dissemination of instructions and menus are crucial. The function (banquet order) sheets must be as complete as possible. There should be no guessing about the size, format, timing, and scope of any functions. Catering software can generate function sheets, production sheets, and equipment lists. The software can also generate recipes with quantities calculated for a specific number of servings.

- If the function sheets are computer generated, the contents should be reviewed and adjusted if necessary. Some computer function sheets have too much useless information.

- The *format* of the function sheets should never vary. Many employees get used to reading only the information that concerns them specifically. If the format changes, they may miss pertinent information.

- Food service workers are pressured for time and need information that is easily understood even by less educated workers.

- Each function sheet must always detail *the day and date* when the function will be held in order to minimize mistakes.

- Function sheets should be completed and posted at least one week in advance. Adjustments, especially the final attendance guarantee, can be made during the week, but the work outline should be available for all to see.

- Each function sheet must be accompanied by a production sheet, detailing the quantities of all items to be produced. There should be no guessing on the part of the kitchen staff. The production sheet is normally made by the person in charge of the kitchen.

- Function sheets should be posted in many production and assembly areas. Nobody should ever have to walk far to get information.

- The name and telephone number of the banquet salesperson who booked the party should be on each sheet in case questions about the function develop.

• Each function sheet must be followed up with an equipment sheet, detailing the exact quantities and types of equipment needed.

• There should be phones in the commissary. Some can be restricted for in-house use.

• Remote phones or radios are essential to stay in contact.

• Functions can be color coded. This is especially useful for off-premise caterers. Each function is assigned a color and colored tape and marking pens are used to identify a party. Every time an item or component is prepared and stored, it is color coded.

• Count, count, and count again. Not getting the right count, and missing a component, can be very frustrating. It is a constant battle to get the right quantities together for each party.

• Sufficient work space is crucial. Banquet food is mass produced and the same techniques used in factories apply in catering kitchens. Table space especially is crucial so items can be produced by a number of workers in an assembly line fashion.

• Wheels are crucial. There should be as many carts and mobile tables as there is space to store them, and as the budget allows.

• Walk in refrigeration is necessary. The floor should be even with the kitchen floor.

• Storage refrigerators should be separate from production refrigerators, which should be used for finished and half-finished products.

• Roll-in cabinets are very useful to keep parties separated. They should be color coded as soon as they are used.

• There should be nonrefrigerated assembly spaces for props, platters, and other items not requiring refrigeration. The equipment placed there should also be identified by the color of the party.

Specific off premise issues

Off premise transportation is a major challenge, but even within large hotels with banquet rooms and kitchens on many floors, transportation can present problems.

• Never book an off premise function without prior site inspection. Investigate parking, access, elevator availability and size, and loading dock. In private homes inquire into access to the service door and whether it will be blocked later by guests. Often electrical circuits do not provide sufficient additional power for heavy cooking equipment, fire codes can prohibit the use of bottled gas in buildings, and smoke alarms can limit the kind of cooking preferred. Frying food in off premise locations is often impossible.

• Provide car phones to stay in contact with drivers.

- Transport in bulk and assemble on site if possible.

- Pack food tightly so it cannot move.

- Pay attention to temperature during transportation. Most items should be transported semifrozen. Insulated transport containers are essential.

- Think about refrigeration on site. In most cases there is very little.

- Bake off or finish on site as much as possible if the space and equipment allow.

- Bring as many carts and rolling tables as possible.

- Always bring a few banquet folding tables along. You can never have too much table space.

- Don't forget tools and plenty of kitchen towels, cleaning rags, and server napkins. An oven and meat thermometers are helpful. Ovens on site quite often do not work properly.

- Don't forget matches. Pilots often do not work.

- Always bring rolls of paper towels, as well as food wrap and foil.

- Be sure to account for soiled equipment, garbage removal, cleanup, and all the other unpleasant aspects of catering. Cleaning supplies should always be on the truck.

- Always have a "strategic reserve" for a fall back situation. Accidents can happen during transport. Braking hard can be a disaster, boxes and trays can be dropped, and many other little disasters can occur. Always have some extra food with you, and keep it frozen if necessary.

- Think about food for the employees. Hungry servers will nibble at food from the platters.

- Take into consideration inclement weather. In-house caterers must have a staffed coat room with sufficient amount of hangers. The doorman and parking lot attendants should have umbrellas to escort customers to their cars. Off-premise caterers should have a contingency plan in case it rains.

The joy of accomplishment

Catering is a wonderful people business. It offers an opportunity to create something and see people enjoying it. It is rewarding to watch customers having a good time and enjoying the result of much planning and work.

BASIC RECIPES

How To Preparation Steps

How to make basic brioche

Brioche is a yeast cake with a high butter and egg content. This recipe must be worked cold and will produce a dense but not fatty product. Although brioche is considered basically a sweet breakfast pastry, it can also be made with little sugar and combined with interesting ingredients. A classical French dish is paté de foie gras (goose liver) baked in brioche.

Traditionally brioche is baked in fluted molds and topped with a little "hat." Brioche dough can be baked in many different molds, including tube molds, which will provide elegant loaves.

Brioche can be served filled by removing the hat and filling the cavity. The dough can be flavored with many interesting ingredients, baked in tiny molds, and served unfilled. This type of brioche is "user friendly" because it does not crumble, is not fatty when picked up, and is easily eaten.

#HT 100   Brioche

Yield: Dependent on application

2 pkg	2 pkg	dry yeast
1 oz	28 g	sugar
½ cup	0.11 l	warm water
36 oz	1.00 kg	flour
10	10	eggs
12 oz	340 g	salted butter or margarine
3 tsp	3 tsp	salt

Combine yeast, sugar, and water. Set aside in warm place to dissolve. In food processor mix butter, eggs, yeast starter, salt, and 1 lb (450 g) flour. Mix well until smooth. Add some additional flour. Put remaining flour on pastry table, add above mixture, and work thoroughly on pastry board until dough is smooth, silky, and all flour is absorbed. Store overnight in refrigerator. Place dough in oiled and floured molds, proof, and bake at 400F°/200°C degrees.

Note: The dough will proof even in the refrigerator. If made to be used the next day it should be frozen and then slowly defrosted in the refrigerator.

Suitable brioche fillings and dough variations are given on pages 121-126.

Step 1 *Ingredients are combined in food processor.*

Step 2 *Mixture is added to flour on pastry table.*

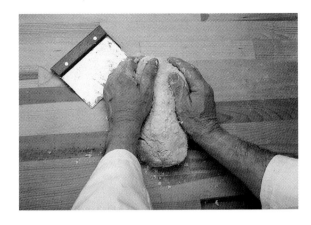

Step 3 *Dough is worked on pastry table.*

How to make cream cheese dough

Cream cheese dough is an easy dough to make that can be baked or fried. The cream cheese adds moisture and flakiness. The dough is best made the day before, stored refrigerated, and worked cold. The dough should be rolled ⅜ in. (10 mm) thick, and can be shaped into triangles to make miniature croissants or into 1 in. (25 mm) circles (silver dollar size). The dough also works well for turnovers, which can be baked or fried.

Cream Cheese Dough   **#HT 101**

Yield: Dependent on application

1 lb	450 g	salted margarine
1 lb	450 g	cream cheese
2	2	egg yolks
18 oz	506 g	cake flour sifted with 1 tbsp baking powder

Combine first three ingredients in bowl or food processor, but do not cream. Add 2 cups (480 g) flour, mix. Place dough on pastry table and work in remaining flour. Keep dough cool.

Note: Cream cheese dough items are suitable for butler style service because the product is not fatty. The items can be made ahead and frozen, and baked when needed. Baked dough also freezes well.

Step 1 *Butter, cream cheese, and egg yolks are combined on pastry table.*

Step 2 *Dough is worked on pastry table. Dough should be kept cool.*

Step 3 *Dough is rolled, cut into 3-in. (75 mm) triangles (for croissants), and filled*

Step 4 *Triangles are rolled to make minicroissants.*

The dough can be modified with any of the following:

- Bacon bits: Add crisp bacon bits according to taste.
- Chili powder: Add ¼ cup (.06 l) chili powder
- Herbs: Add ½ cup (.12 l) chopped herbs consisting of parsley, chives, thyme, sage, and rosemary.
- Paprika: Add ¼ cup (.06 l) Hungarian paprika.
- Poppy seeds: Add ½ cup (.12 l) poppy seeds.
- Sunflower seeds: Add coarsely chopped salted sunflower seeds.

Cream cheese dough items, recipe #HT 101, page 29, during production with various toppings, here and in the picture below.

How to Make Filo (Strudel) Dough

Filo dough is available frozen, ready to use, in very thin, almost transparent sheets, in 1 lb (450 g) packages. For best results, the dough should be defrosted in the refrigerator. Since the filo sheets ares very thin, they will dry quickly when exposed to room temperature. The dough sheets should be worked on a damp cloth, and the sheets not being used immediately should be kept covered.

Filo dough can also be made on premise. It is often referred to as pulled Strudel dough, because the large sheets are used in Austria to make Strudel. It is also commonly spelled *phyllo*.

#HT 102 Filo (Strudel) Dough (Homemade)

Yield: Dependent on application

24 oz	675 g	bread flour
1½ oz	0.04 l	oil
2	2	eggs
1½ cups	0.35 l	warm water

Combine ingredients on pastry board to make a soft dough. The dough must be worked very hard and long to develop the gluten in the flour. Cover and let rest 1 hour before using it.

The dough cannot be rolled by conventional means. It must be stretched by hand on a lightly floured tablecloth until transparent. This takes a certain amount of practice.

How to work with purchased filo dough

Filo dough is available in packages and is rolled into thin sheets, ready to use. Filo dough is fat free and must be brushed with melted butter or oil to keep the layers flaky and separated. When baked, filo dough items should be flaky but not oily.

Pan spray can be used to reduce the fat content, but it is not advisable to replace butter or oil completely.

The filo sheets used in these illustrations are 14 x 18 in. (35 x 450 mm).

Step 1 *One sheet of filo dough is placed on a damp cloth, brushed with butter, and covered with a second sheet. The filo sheets are cut with a pie cutter into 16 pieces.*

Step 2 *The pieces are filled and folded into bundles, with the seam side down. They will be brushed with melted butter before baking.*

Step 3 *Filling in progress. If the filling is smooth, a pastry bag can be used.*

Step 4 *Fill dough with different fillings. From right to left: #R 130 blue cheese, cream cheese, apples and walnut, #R 134 cauliflower filling (vegetarian), #R 144 smoked trout and spinach, and #R 138 pancetto (Italian bacon) and savoy cabbage.*

Filo items can be shaped many different ways. These pictures show 1½ x 1 in. (37 x 25 mm) bundles, because they are quickly made and easy to eat. The same technique can be used to make triangles (called *tiropetes* in Greek), turnovers, strudels, and nests. When using different fillings it might be advantageous to differentiate the items by shape.

Strudels are filled sheets rolled into a long tube and cut after baking. Strudels are much faster to make than individual pieces. To make strudels place double sheets of filo on a moist towel, dab with melted butter. Form filling into 1 in. (25 mm) tube (best done when filling is cold) and place at end of dough closer to you. Roll tightly, place strudel on baking sheet, and brush with butter.

Strudels are attractive to look at because the filling is exposed, but are messy to eat when passed butler style because the fillings can fall out. If fillings are loose, tighten with fresh bread crumbs and adjust seasoning accordingly.

We recommend making strudel-type hors d'oeuvres with flaky cheese dough.

Filo nests are made by placing three squares of dough into oiled muffin or tartlet molds. The dough is brushed inside with butter and filled with dry beans to prevent the dough from collapsing during baking. The shells can be filled with a wide variety of fillings after baking, or baked with the filling inside. Filo nests are available commercially, ready to use in 3 in. (75 mm) and bite-size minishells.

How to Make Flaky Yeast Dough

Flaky yeast dough is a short (flaky) dough that does not need proofing. After the yeast has dissolved in warm water it is added to the remaining ingredients and worked on the pastry table like a bread dough. The dough must be kept cold.

#HT 103

Flaky Yeast Dough

Yield: 140 round pieces 1½ in. (37 mm) across

1 pkg	1 pkg	dry yeast
½ cup	0.11 l	milk
1 tbsp	1 tbsp	sugar
22 oz	615 g	bread flour
8 oz	225 g	butter or margarine
2	2	egg yolks
½ tsp	½ tsp	salt

Dilute yeast with sugar in small amount of warm milk. Put flour on pastry board, place fats, egg yolks, and salt in center well, add diluted yeast and make dough. Add milk as needed. The dough should be stiff and well worked. Wrap in plastic and refrigerate before use. This yeast dough does not need proofing.

Note: The dough can be shaped into circles, triangles, turnovers, and strudels. It is especially suitable for miniature pizzas.

Step 1 *The diluted yeast is added to other ingredients on the pastry board.*

Step 2 *The dough is worked.*

Step 3 *In this application the dough is rolled out and cut into 1½ in. (37 mm) circles (silver dollars).*

How to Make Pate Brisée (Shell Dough)

This is the standard dough for tartlets, quiche, paté, and many other uses. The dough is not as interesting as other varieties, but it is a good stand-by for many applications.

Shell Dough   **#HT 104**

Yield: 60 small tartlets

12 oz	350 g	salted butter or margarine
20 oz	560 g	cake flour
2	2	egg yolks
4 tbsp	4 tbsp	cold water
1 tsp	1 tsp	baking powder

Note: Dry spices can be added to the dough during the mixing process according to taste, such as chili powder, curry, tumeric, soy sauce (instead of water), cracked pepper. A small amount of sugar (about 1 tsp) will help brown the product for tartlets and quiche.

The dough can be modified by adding any of the following:

• Parmesan: Add 1 cup (0.23 l) grated Parmesan cheese when making dough.

• Coriander: Put 6 tbsp crushed coriander seeds in dry frying pan and toast until light brown. Chill. Crush. Add to ingredients when making dough.

Step 1 *Combine all ingredients on baker's table.*

Step 2 *Work dough. Let dough rest in refrigerator before use.*

Step 3 *Roll dough and fill tartlet molds.*

Step 4 *Fill mold with beans or rice, blind bake.*

Open Sandwiches

#HT 105 ## How to Work with Open Sandwiches

Open sandwiches can be topped with many different fillings and quickly broiled before service. They are then cut into attractive shapes. It is efficient to work with bread slices lengthwise. The breads used in these illustrations were 4 loaves made by Fink Baking Company in Long Island City, New York

Many fillings and toppings can be used and there is no limit to the imagination. Using bread sliced lengthwise cuts down production time considerably.

Note: If desired, the smoked salmon can also be put on the bread first, and then covered with fish mousse. This method prevents the smoked salmon

Step 1 *For efficiency, use bread sliced lengthwise. The breads shown (from the bottom) are whole wheat, white, and rye.*

Step 2 *Spread filling on breads. The fillings shown are (from the bottom):*

On white bread: shrimp spread, recipe #R 143, page 61.

On white bread: smoked salmon and dill on top of fish mousse, recipe #R 136, page 58.

On rye bread: poultry mousse, recipe #R 140, page 60, with sun-dried tomato pesto. The pesto is best purchased ready to use from a reputable supplier.

Step 3 *The sandwiches are baked/broiled at 500°F/ 260°C degrees for about 5 to 8 minutes. The sandwiches are allowed to cool and are cut into attractive pieces.*

from drying out. The sun-dried tomato pesto can make the bread soggy. The bread can be spread first with poultry mousse and then brushed with sun-dried tomato pesto. Apply poultry mousse generously because it will shrink.

Rice Wafer Paper

How to Work with Rice Wafer Paper   **#HT 106**

Rice wafer paper is available in thin, flavorless 8½ x 11 in. (210 x 275 mm) sheets and is sold through pastry supply purveyors. The paper is brittle but will soften when moist. It will dissolve when wet. It is used to keep soft food together until cooked.

Step 1 Assemble tools and ingredients: rice wafer paper, scissors, brush, and cold water.

Step 2 Cut paper into suitable pieces with scissors. Place on moist (not wet) surface.

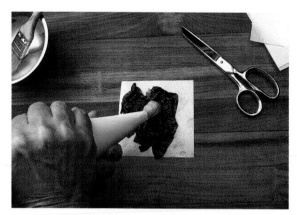

Step 3 Use pastry bag to add filling if applicable. In this application, chicken mousse was added to a spinach filling.

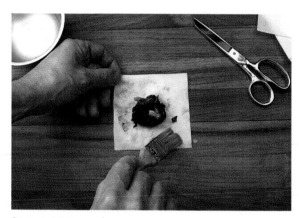

Step 4 Moisten edges.

Step 5 Wrap paper around filling into neat bundle. Place on oiled sheet and refrigerate or freeze. The product can be steamed or grilled but must be oiled to prevent sticking and burning.

Note: The paper is soft and difficult to handle before and after steaming. The product must be placed in a well-oiled steamer basket and is not easily removed right after it has been steamed. As soon as the product has cooled somewhat it can be handled quite well. When the product is grilled, it must be well brushed with oil to prevent sticking. It will firm up after grilling.

Basic Recipes for Cold Canapes

The recipes are organized alphabetically and start with the number #RC 50.

Green Hot Sauce   #RC 50

Yield: 3 cups (0.7 l)

2 cups	0.46 l	chopped green peppers (seeded)
1 cup	0.23 l	avocado pulp
1 tbsp	1 tbsp	prepared mustard
2 tbsp	2 tbsp	white vinegar
¼ cup	0.06 l	mayonnaise
		Jalapeño pepper, chopped, to taste
		salt and pepper, to taste

Process all ingredients to a fine puree.

Marinated Eggplant Spread   #RC 51

Yield: Dependent on application

½ cup	0.11 l	olive oil
1 tsp	1 tsp	minced garlic
1 tsp	1 tsp	minced basil leaves
1 tsp	1 tsp	oregano, ground
		juice of 1 lemon
		salt and pepper to taste
10 oz	300 g	eggplants (2 small)

Combine all ingredients except eggplants. Peel eggplant and cut into 1 in. (25 mm) slices. Marinate overnight in oil and spice mixture. Broil until brown on both sides. Chill and puree.

#RC 52

Oriental Egg Omelette

Yield: Dependent on application

6	6	eggs, beaten
8 tbsp	8 tbsp	dashi (bonito soup)
½ tsp	½ tsp	salt
1 tsp	1 tsp	light soy sauce
1 tsp	1 tsp	mirin or sake
1 tbsp	1 tbsp	sugar
2 tbsp	2 tbsp	salad oil

Optional garnishes:
- toasted black sesame seeds
- grated daikon
- sweet vinegar ginger

Blend ingredients thoroughly. Make thin pancakes in hot black skillet. Roll pancakes into tight rolls while still warm.

Note: Oriental chefs use a square skillet and roll the pancakes in special bamboo mats.

#RC 53

Pimento Spread

Yield: 2 cups (0.46 l)

4	4	large red peppers
1 tbsp	1 tbsp	honey
2 tbsp	2 tbsp	vinegar
¼ cup	0.06 l	red wine
		juice of 1 lemon
¼ cup	0.06 l	olive oil
		salt and pepper to taste

Peel peppers by exposing to heat; wash and remove seeds. Cut in pieces and simmer with remaining ingredients until soft. Puree in food processor.

Note: There are many methods of peeling peppers. They can be put in deep fat fryers until the peel blisters off, or oiled and place under the broiler. Also exposing the peppers to direct heat—such as a gas flame—will remove the skin. Regardless of which process is used, the peppers must be washed in warm water to remove all fat and any black spots. Canned pimentos can be substituted.

Smoked Salmon Spread

Yield: 120 canapes

2 lb	900 g	smoked salmon, skin removed
1 cup	0.23 l	sour cream
2 tbsp	2 tbsp	dill, chopped

Make sure all bones are removed from salmon; small bones in the fillet must be removed with pliers. Puree fish in food processor with sour cream and dill. Refrigerate overnight before use.

Note: Mousse is more interesting when the puree is mixed with a small amount of diced salmon to enhance texture and appearance.

Smoked Salmon Tartare

#RC 55

Yield: 120 canapes

1 lb	450 g	smoked salmon fillets, skinless
1 lb	450 g	salmon fillet, skinless, (very fresh!)
1	1	lemon
1 ¾ oz	0.05 l	olive oil
2 tbsp	2 tbsp	dill, chopped
2 tbsp	2 tbsp	shallots, chopped
2 tbsp	2 tbsp	capers, chopped
		salt and coarsely ground pepper to taste

Remove all bones from salmon fillets. Chop fish with sharp knife. *Do not squash fish!* Fish should not be mushy. Grate lemon and add peel to fish. Add all remaining ingredients, season with salt and pepper.

#RC 56

Smoked Trout Spread

Yield: Dependent on application

1 lb	450 g	*trout fillets, boneless and skinless*
½ cup	0.11 l	*sour cream*
1 tbsp	1 tbsp	*horseradish*
		salt and pepper to taste

Puree all ingredients in food processor. If mixture is too thick, dilute with sour cream.

#RC 57

Tuna Tartare

Yield: 120 canapes

2 lb	900 g	*tuna fillet,* skinless (very fresh!)
2½ oz	0.10 l	*olive oil*
2 tbsp	2 tbsp	*shallots, chopped*
2 tbsp	2 tbsp	*capers, chopped*
1 tbsp	2 tbsp	*anchovy, chopped*
1 tbsp	1 tbsp	*parsley, chopped*
2 tbsp	2 tbsp	*Teryaki sauce*
		salt and coarsely ground pepper to taste

Chop fish with sharp knife. *Do not squash fish!* Fish should not be mushy. Add all remaining ingredients, season with salt and pepper.

* The taste, fat content, and density of flesh varies greatly between the size of the fish and the location of the cut used. For eye appeal the tuna flesh should have dark marks, and for Western taste the flesh should not be very fatty. Tail pieces, well trimmed are most suitable. Belly and back pieces can be fatty.

Vegetable Terrine

Yield: 100

4 cups	0.92 l	cauliflower florets
2 cups	0.46 l	carrots, chopped
2 cups	0.46 l	frozen small peas
3 oz	85 g	cream cheese
3	3	eggs, separated
1 tbsp	1 tbsp	chives, chopped
2 tbsp	2 tbsp	ground almonds
¼ tsp	¼ tsp	nutmeg
1 tsp	1 tsp	lemon juice
		salt and pepper to taste

Steam cauliflower and carrots until cooked, but not mushy. In food processor puree each vegetable separately with 1 oz (28 g) cream cheese and one egg yolk. Add chives to peas and season to taste. Add almonds to carrots and season to taste. Add nutmeg to cauliflower and season to taste. Whip egg whites to stiff foam and blend into vegetable purees. Fill suitable ceramic or Pyrex molds with layers of vegetable purees and bake in water bath for about 45 minutes or until firm.

Basic Recipes for Hors d'Oeuvres

The recipes are organized alphabetically and start with the number #R 106.

Batters and dough

#R 106

Biscuits, Baking Powder

Yield: 100 pieces

18 oz	500 g	cake flour
2 tbsp	2 tbsp	baking powder
6 oz	170 g	salted margarine
1	1	egg
1 cup	0.23 l	milk
1 tsp	1 tsp	salt

Sift together flour and baking powder. Blend eggs, milk, and salt. Mix flour mixture and margarine, add egg mixture to form soft dough. Roll ½ in. (13 mm) thick, cut into rounds or other shapes. Bake at 400°F/200°C.

Note: Add liquid slowly because the absorbency of flour varies. The dough should be workable on the bench. Southern biscuits are famous because they are made with soft flour.

Note: Wet and dry biscuit mixes can be purchased ready to use but are often too sweet for hors d'oeuvres.

#R 107

Cream Puff or Eclair Paste

Yield: 60 puffs

32 oz	0.92 l	milk
1 tsp	1 tsp	salt
½ tsp	½ tsp	nutmeg
16 oz	450 g	butter or margarine
24 oz	670 g	flour, sifted
20	20	eggs

Bring milk, salt, nutmeg, and butter to boil. Add flour at once and stir over heat until mixture is smooth and does not stick to sides of the pot. Remove from heat. Add eggs one by one, stirring continuously. This is best done with an electric mixer (use paddle) or in a food processor, pulse on/off.

Six varieties of biscuits. Starting clockwise with the green herb biscuits #H 108, page 119; parmesan biscuits #H 110, page 120; poppy seed biscuits #H 111, page 120; cheddar biscuits #H 104, page 117; hazelnut biscuits #H 107, page 119; and bacon biscuits #H 102, page 116.

Note: This dough can be fried or baked. It should be piped while still warm. The dough can be flavored with spices and different cheeses. The paste should be cool before a stringy cheese is added.

Empanada Blue Corn Dough   #R 108

Yield: Dependent on application

14 oz	400 g	blue cornmeal
6 oz	170 g	flour
1 tbsp	1 tbsp	baking powder
1 tbsp	1 tbsp	chili powder
½ cup	0.11 l	oil
16 oz	0.46 l	water

Sift cornmeal, flour, baking powder, and chili powder together. Place in bowl and add oil and cold water. Work to a stiff dough.

Note: The dough should be used right away. The dough is best shaped with wet hands. It will become very solid when the cornmeal starts to absorb the water. When the dough is too solid, it can be broken up in the electric mixer, using a paddle and a small amount of cold water can be added.

#R 109

Empanada Curry Dough

Yield: About 40

24 oz	675 g	flour
1 tbsp	1 tbsp	baking powder
2 tbsp	2 tbsp	curry powder
8 oz	225 g	shortening
¾ cup	0.17 l	cold water

Combine ingredients to stiff dough. Work cold.

#R 110

Empanada Masa Harina Dough

Yield: 60

2 cups	0.46 l	masa harina flour
2 cups	0.46 l	flour
3½ cups	0.80 l	water
8 oz	0.225 g	shortening
4	4	eggs
1 tsp	1 tsp	turmeric
1 tsp	1 tsp	cumin
¼ tsp	¼ tsp	cayenne pepper
		salt to taste

Combine ingredients in food processor. Chill. Dough can be baked or fried.

#R 111

Frying Batter with Beer

Yield: About 100 pieces

24 oz	0.70 l	(2 cans) beer
5 cups	1.15 l	flour, sifted
½ pkg	½ pkg	dry yeast
		salt to taste
2 tbsp	2 tbsp	oil
4	4	egg whites

Combine beer with flour, yeast, salt, and oil. The paste will be very thick but will thin out due to fermentation. Cover and let rest at room temperature for 4 hours. Beat egg whites until soft peaks form and fold into batter. If batter is too thick to handle dilute with a little warm water.

Frying Batter, Tempura

#R 112

Yield: 50 pieces

1	1	egg
2 cups	0.46 l	ice water
8 oz	0.225 g	flour

Combine ingredients and mix well. Use chopsticks to dip vegetables in batter.

Note: This batter is very thin and the vegetables will be quite visible under the coating when fried.

Frying Batter with Wine

#R 113

Yield: About 80 pieces

16 oz	0.46 l	dry white wine
1 cup	0.23 l	water
2 tbsp	2 tbsp	oil
1 tsp	1 tsp	sugar
4½ cups	0.90 l	flour
2	2	egg whites

Combine wine with oil, water, sugar, and flour. Cover and let refrigerate 2 hours. Beat egg whites until soft peaks form and fold into batter.

Frying Batter with Yeast

#R 114

Yield: Dependent on application

2 cups	0.46 l	milk
1 pkg	1 pkg	dry yeast
1 tsp	1 tsp	sugar
2 cups	0.46 l	bread flour
2	2	eggs
1 tbsp	1 tbsp	oil
1 tsp	1 tsp	salt

Warm milk to 100°F/40°C degrees, add yeast and sugar. Cover and let rest in warm spot until yeast is dissolved. Add remaining ingredients and mix until smooth and thoroughly mixed. Cover and let proof on warm spot until batter has risen.

#R 115

Basic Kasha

Yield: 4 cups (0.90 l)

1 lb	450 g	kasha
2	2	eggs
½ cup	0.23 l	shortening
4 cups	0.92 l	water

Break eggs, mix, and combine dry with kasha. This is best done by rubbing and crumbling the kernels. The purpose is to coat the kasha kernels evenly with egg. Add shortening to hot water to melt, add mixture to kasha. Bring to boil, cover, and cook over low heat until all water is absorbed, or about 50 minutes. Spread cooked kasha in a tray to cool.

#R 116

Basic Corn Muffin

Yield: 50 pieces

3 cups	0.70 l	coarse cornmeal
3 cups	0.70 l	flour
2½ tbsp	2½ tbsp	baking powder
1 tbsp	1 tbsp	salt
1 tsp	1 tsp	white pepper, ground
1 tsp	1 tsp	tumeric, ground
6	6	eggs
3 cups	0.70 l	milk
1 cup	0.23 l	oil
		salt and pepper

Combine dry ingredients, mix in wet ingredients, and stir well. Bake at 400°F/200°C.

Note: Mixture can be baked in sheet pans, or in muffin cups. Ready to use dry mixes or batters are often too sweet to use as hors d'oeuvres.

Blue Corn Muffins

#R 117

Yield: 80 pieces

10 oz	280 g	cake flour
12 oz	340 g	blue cornmeal
2 tsp	2 tsp	baking powder
8 oz	225 g	butter or margarine, melted
4	4	eggs
16 oz	0.46 l	buttermilk
½ cup	0.11 l	milk
1 tsp	1 tsp	salt

Combine dry ingredients. Mix wet ingredients. Combine both to make batter. Do not whip.

Muffins with Poppy Seeds

#R 118

Yield: 50 Pieces

16 oz	450 g	cake flour
8 oz	225 g	poppy seeds
1 tsp	1 tsp	baking powder
6 oz	170 g	butter or margarine, melted
2	2	eggs
1 cup	0.23 l	buttermilk

Combine dry ingredients. Mix wet ingredients. Combine both to make batter. Do not whip.

#R 119   ## Basic Pie Dough

Yield: Dependent on application

1 tbsp	1 tbsp	salt
1 tbsp	1 tbsp	sugar
1½ cups	0.34 l	ice water (variable)
24 oz	670 g	cake flour
8 oz	225 g	bread flour
8 oz	225 g	butter
16 oz	450 g	shortening

Dissolve salt and sugar in water. Mix flour, butter, and shortening until crumbly. Add cold water, mix as little as possible, just enough to make dough. Put on pastry board. roll into ball, cover, and refrigerate.

#R 120   ## Pie Dough with Cheddar Cheese

Yield: Dependent on application

16 oz	450 g	shortening
8 oz	225 g	butter
24 oz	670 g	cake flour
8 oz	225 g	bread flour
1 tbsp	1 tbsp	sugar
1 lb	450 g	sharp cheddar cheese, grated
1 tbsp	1 tbsp	salt
1 tbsp	1 tbsp	paprika
1½ cups	0.34 l	ice water (variable)

Dissolve salt in water. Mix flour, butter, paprika, sugar, and shortening until crumbly, but not creamed. Add cheese and cold water, mix as little as possible, just enough to make dough. Put on pastry board, roll into ball, cover, and refrigerate.

Polenta

#R 121

Yield: Dependent on application

16 oz	0.46 l	milk
16 oz	0.46 l	chicken stock
9 oz	250 g	coarse cornmeal
2	2	egg yolks
1 cup	0.23 l	Parmesan cheese

Combine milk and chicken stock, bring to boil. Add cornmeal while mixing with wire whisk. Cover pot and cook over slow heat for 20 minutes. Add egg yolks and cheese and spread mixture about ½ in. (12 mm) high on oiled sheet pan. Cover with foil and refrigerate overnight.

Note: Coarse cornmeal is available in Hispanic stores and in health food stores. Regular corn meal can be substituted.

Popovers

#R 122

Yield: 50

12 oz	340 g	flour
6	6	eggs
4 cups	0.92 l	light cream
1 tbsp	1 tbsp	Worcestershire sauce
1 tsp	1 tsp	chili powder
		oil

Combine all ingredients, but do not whip. Strain batter to remove any lumps. Refrigerate 1 hour before use. Fill tiny muffin tins ¼ in. (7 mm) with oil. Place tins on sheet pan in 500°F/260°C oven and heat until oil is smoking hot. Pour batter into each tin and fill about three-fourths full. Return to oven at once and bake until brown and fluffy.

Note: Popovers were originally made with hot beef fat when roasting meat. The fat gave a wonderful flavor to the popovers, but this is no longer acceptable because of dietary concerns. Oil is used as substitute. Popovers must be baked all the way through, otherwise they will collapse. If necessary they can be dried in a medium hot oven.

Note: Popovers are hollow cakes baked in small muffin tins. They can be flavored with spices, such as chili powder, curry, crab seasoning, and many others.

#R 123

Potato Dough

Yield: Dependent on application

40 oz	1.12 kg	Russet potatoes
12 oz	335 g	bread flour
4	4	egg yolks
pinch	pinch	nutmeg
		salt, to taste

Bake or boil potatoes until done, peel while still hot and press through food mill or ricer. This must be done while potatoes are still hot. Place potatoes on pastry board and let cool. Make well in center, add eggs and spices. Make stiff dough by working in flour. The dough should be stiff; add more flour if needed.

#R 124

Potato Cheese Dough

Follow recipe #R 123 Potato Dough and add 1 cup (0.23 l) grated Parmesan cheese to recipe.

#R 125

Semolina Gnocchi

Yield: 50

16 oz	0.46 l	milk
16 oz	0.46 l	chicken stock
9 oz	250 g	coarse semolina
2	2	egg yolks
1 cup	0.23 l	Parmesan cheese

Combine milk and chicken stock, bring to boil. Add semolina while mixing with wire whisk. Cover pot and cook over slow heat 20 minutes. Add egg yolks and cheese and spread mixture about ½ in. (12 mm) high on oiled sheet pan. Cover with foil and refrigerate overnight. Cut into attractive pieces and grill or fry.

Note: Semolina is coarse cream of wheat. If semolina is not available, cream of wheat can be substituted.

Sushi Rice

#R 126

Yield: 4 cups (0.92 l)

3⅓ cups	0.75 l	okome, short grain Japanese rice
4 cups	0.92 l	water
4 tbsp	4 tbsp	salt
½ cup	0.11 l	sushi vinegar
5 tbsp	5 tbsp	sugar

Wash rice until water runs clean. Drain. Add water and salt, bring to boil covered and simmer for about 10 minutes. Let rest covered about for 10 minutes. Mix vinegar with sugar and bring to boil. Cool. Spread rice to cool and blend in vinegar. The cooked rice should be room temperature when used.

Note: Electric rice cookers are practical and worth the investment if rice is prepared frequently.

Wild Rice

#R 127

Yield: 2 cups (0.46 l)

1 cup	0.23 l	wild rice
1 tbsp	1 tbsp	onions, chopped
1 tbsp	1 tbsp	oil
2 cups	0.46 l	water
		salt to taste

Soak wild rice overnight, drain and discard water. Saute onions in oil, add wild rice and water. Salt to taste. Cover, bring to boil, simmer 30 minutes. Remove lid and let steam escape for 5 minutes over low heat. Empty on sheet pan to cool.

#R 128

Wonton Dough with Eggs

Yield: 80–100 3 x 3 in. (75 x 75 mm) pieces

3	3	eggs
3 cups	0.70 l	flour
3 tbsp	3 tbsp	water

Combine ingredients and make stiff dough. Let rest in refrigerator before use.

Fillings for baked items

#R 129

Beef Filling for Turnovers (Empanadas)

Yield: Filling for 50 turnovers

16 oz	450 g	lean beef, ground
1 tbsp	1 tbsp	oil
½ cup	0.11 l	onions, chopped
½ tbsp	½ tbsp	garlic, chopped
1½ tsp	1½ tsp	cumin, ground
¼ tsp	¼ tsp	tabasco sauce
1 cup	0.23 l	tomatoes, chopped
4 tsp	4 tsp	chives, chopped
2 tbsp	2 tbsp	flour or masa harina flour

Brown meat in skillet over slow heat, stirring frequently to break up meat into small, crumbly pieces. When meat is cooked, drain off fat, add oil, and saute onions and garlic. Add remaining ingredients, bring to boil and season to taste.

Note: Mixture is best used while still at room temperature.

Blue Cheese, Cream Cheese, Apples, and Walnuts   **#R 130**

Yield: Filling for 60 pieces

8 oz	225 g	cream cheese
8 oz	225 g	blue cheese
2 cups	0.46 l	apples,* peeled and diced
4 oz	112 g	walnuts, chopped

Combine ingredients. The apples should be diced very fine, and a little red skin should be left on for color.

Note: Suitable for baking on rice wafer paper.

* Red delicious apples are preferred.

Blue Cheese, Apples, and Walnuts   **#R 131**

Yield: Filling for 60 pieces

3	3	golden delicious apples, size 100
16 oz	450 g	blue cheese, crumbled
1 cup	0.23 l	fresh bread crumbs
8 oz	225 g	walnuts, chopped

Peel apples, cut in quarters, core. Combine all ingredients.

Note: Bread crumbs are added to absorb fat when the cheese melts. The amount of bread crumbs needed varies. This filling can be used with cream cheese dough and with filo dough. When used in tartlets, the mixture should be baked until the cheese melts.

#R 132   Brie Cheese and Sun-dried Tomato Pesto

Yield: 50

16 oz	*450 g*	*brie, ripe, but not runny*
4 oz	*112 g*	*sun-dried tomato pesto**

* The pesto is best purchased ready to use from a reputable supplier.

Depending on ripeness, cut cheese in little slivers and top with pesto when used, or mash cheese with pesto. Use in cream cheese dough items, filo items, and in tartlets (heat in tartlets).

#R 133   Cabbage and Dill

Yield: about 50 croissants

16 oz	*450 g*	*green cabbage*
½ cup	*0.11 l*	*oil*
½ cup	*0.11 l*	*onions, chopped*
1 tsp	*1 tsp*	*dill seeds, chopped*
1 tsp	*1 tsp*	*salt*
½ tsp	*½ tsp*	*butcher ground pepper*
½ cup	*½ cup*	*dill, chopped*

Coarsely chop cabbage, wash well, and drain. Saute onions in oil, add remaining ingredients and 1 cup (0.23 l) water, cover and braise 30 minutes over low heat. Occasionally a little water must be added. The mixture should be cooked, but should have very little residual moisture. Remove from heat, drain if necessary, chop coarsely in food processor.

Cauliflower Filling (vegetarian)   #R 134

Yield: 50

¼ cup	0.06 l	red peppers, diced small
2 tbsp	2 tbsp	onions, chopped
1 tbsp	1 tbsp	oil
3 tbsp	3 tbsp	parsley, chopped
½ tsp	½ tsp	pepper, ground
1 tbsp	1 tbsp	flour
1½ cups	0.35 l	cauliflower, cooked and chopped
2 tbsp	2 tbsp	olive oil
¼ tsp	¼ tsp	cumin
1 tbsp	1 tbsp	salt

Boil diced peppers 3 minutes, drain. Saute onions in 1 tbsp oil until limp, add parsley and pepper, set aside. Sprinkle flour over cauliflower and blend. Heat 2 tbsp oil in heavy pan and saute cauliflower until some pieces are light brown. Add remaining ingredients and mix well.

Note: By sauteing the cauliflower moisture will be removed and the flavor enhanced.

Colombian Empanada Filling   #R 135

Yield: 50 pieces

½ cup	0.11 l	raisins, seedless
32 oz	900 g	beef, ground
1 cup	0.23 l	onions, chopped
2 tbsp	2 tbsp	chili powder
3	3	hard boiled eggs, chopped
1 tbsp	1 tbsp	cilantro, chopped
		salt to taste

Soak raisins in cold water. Cook meat and onions in slow oven, stirring and breaking up pieces. Mixture should be brown and crumbly. Drain off fat, add drained raisins and all remaining ingredients. Blend and cool. Form half moon shaped turnovers, fill, close tightly, and refrigerate. Empanadas can be baked or fried.

#R 136

Fish Mousse

Yield: Dependent on application

16 oz	450 g	solid fish, such as halibut, sole, pike, scallops, or salmon
3	3	egg whites
1 cup	0.23 l	36 percent heavy cream
1 tbsp	1 tbsp	salt
1 tbsp	1 tbsp	white pepper, ground

Make sure fish is very cold/almost frozen. Grind through fine blade of meat grinder and mix in food processor with all ingredients. Be careful not to overheat.*

* Use pulse on/off.

#R 137

Lamb and Pignoli

Yield: Filling for 100–150

6 oz	0.23 l	pignoli (pine nuts)
32 oz	900 g	lamb, ground
1 cup	0.23 l	onions, diced
½ tsp	½ tsp	garlic
		curry or masala paste to taste
1 tbsp	1 tbsp	flour
		salt and cayenne pepper to taste
¼ cup	0.06 l	fresh mint leaves, chopped

Toast pignoli in oven until light brown. Chop coarsely. Cook lamb in non-stick skillet until brown and crumbly. Frequent stirring is necessary to break up pieces. Drain off fat. Add onions, garlic, and curry or masala paste. Stir well and cook over low heat until ingredients are well mixed. Sprinkle with flour, add ¾ cup (0.18 l) water, bring to boil and cook to thick paste. Season to taste, add pignoli nuts, and mint leaves.

Note: This filling is suitable for turnovers, tartlets, and as topping on silver dollars.

Pancetta (Italian Bacon) and Savoy Cabbage

Yield: Filling for about 50 croissants

20 oz	563 g	savoy cabbage
6 oz	168 g	pancetta, ground or cut in very small dice
½ cup	0.11 l	oil
½ cup	0.11 l	onions, chopped
1 tsp	1 tsp	caraway seeds, chopped
1 tsp	1 tsp	salt
½ tsp	½ tsp	butcher ground pepper

Coarsely chop savoy cabbage, wash thoroughly, and drain. Saute pancetta and onions in oil, add remaining ingredients and 1 cup (0.23 l) water, cover and braise 30 minutes over low heat. Occasionally a little water must be added. The mixture should be cooked, but should have very little residual moisture. Remove from heat, drain if necessary, chop coarsely in food processor.

Pork Filling with Anise

Yield: 100 pieces

32 oz	900 g	pork, ground
32 oz	900 g	anise (fennel)
1 tbsp	1 tbsp	flour
		salt and butcher ground black pepper to taste

Cook pork in nonstick skillet until brown and crumbly. Frequent stirring is necessary to break up pieces. Drain off fat. In the meantime, clean anise, and save some greens. Cut anise bulbs into chunks and chop in food processor into small pieces. Use on/off pulse and make sure all pieces are chopped about evenly. Add anise to pork, season with salt and pepper, cover and cook over low heat until the vegetables is cooked, but still crisp. Sprinkle with flour and add a little water if necessary to make thick filling. Chop fennel leaves and add to filling.

#R 140 | # Poultry Mousse

Yield: Dependent on application

20 oz	560 g	boneless and skinless chicken meat, ground or turkey, ground
3	3	egg whites
1 cup	0.23 l	36 percent heavy cream
¼ tsp	¼ tsp	nutmeg, ground
½ tbsp	½ tbsp	salt
1 tbsp	1 tbsp	white pepper, ground

Make sure meat is very cold/almost frozen. Grind through fine blade of meat grinder (if applicable) and mix all ingredients in food processor. Be careful not to overheat.*

* Use on/off pulse.

Note: Mousse is best shaped by piping it with a pastry bag into ¾ in. (18 mm) cylinders. After chilling or freezing the cylinders can be cut into 1 in. (25 mm) sections.

#R 141 | # Oysters Rockefeller

Yield: 80

1 qt	0.93 l	shucked oysters
½ cup	0.11 l	pine nuts
3 tbsp	3 tbsp	oil
3 tbsp	3 tbsp	onions, chopped
1/8 tsp	1/8 tsp	garlic, chopped
1 cup	0.23 l	spinach, cooked and chopped
8 oz	225 g	Swiss cheese
3 oz	0.09 l	Pernod
		salt and pepper

Bring oysters in their own juice to boiling point and cool. When cold, drain oysters, save juice. Chop oysters into coarse pieces and chill. Saute pine nuts in oil until light brown, add onions and garlic. Cook until onions are translucent. Add oyster juice, but make sure the sand which has accumulated on the bottom is discarded. Add spinach, cheese, and Pernod. Cook until thoroughly heated. Cool and combine with oysters. Season to taste.

Note: Frozen chopped spinach works fine in this recipe. If filling is very wet, thicken with fresh bread crumbs.

Seafood Oriental Filling

Yield: Filling for 125 tartlets

16 oz	450 g	raw shrimp, PDQ, any size or broken pieces
16 oz	450 g	scallops, any size
2 tbsp	2 tbsp	black sesame oil
2 tbsp	2 tbsp	oil
1 tbsp	1 tbsp	garlic, chopped
½ cup	0.11 l	green onions (scallion), chopped
1 tbsp	1 tbsp	ginger, chopped
1 tsp	1 tsp	Thai shrimp paste (Kapi)
2 cups	0.46 l	bok choy, chopped
1 cup	0.23 l	water chestnuts, drained and chopped

Wash shrimp and scallops, drain. Chop coarsely in food processor, do not puree. Combine with sesame oil, set aside. Saute in oil garlic, green onions and ginger, add shrimp paste and bok choy. Cook over high heat until cabbage is wilted, add water chestnuts. Cool and combine with seafood mixture.

Note: Scallops can have shell particles and therefore should be carefully checked before use.

Shrimp Spread for Fillings or Toast

Yield: 40

16 oz	450 g	raw shrimp, shelled and cleaned, any size
¼ cup	0.06 l	mirin
¼ cup	0.06 l	cold water
1 tbsp	1 tbsp	cornstarch
1 tsp	1 tsp	paprika
1 tsp	1 tsp	salt
½ tsp	½ tsp	white pepper, ground

Make sure shrimp are well washed in cold water. Drain. Process all ingredients in food processor. Do not overmix; the filling should be slightly coarse.

#R 144

Smoked Trout and Spinach Filling

Yield: 80

4 (8–10 oz each)	4 (225–280 g each)	smoked trout
1 cup	0.23 l	frozen spinach or fresh spinach, cooked and chopped
1 tbsp	1 tbsp	olive oil
1 tbsp	1 tbsp	onions, chopped
¼ tsp	¼ tsp	garlic, chopped
½ tsp	½ tsp	black pepper, ground
¼ tsp	¼ tsp	nutmeg, ground
1 tsp	1 tsp	salt
1 cup	0.23 l	Swiss cheese, diced small

Remove skin and bone trout. This is best done when fish is at room temperature. Flake and remove all bones, making sure hairline, thin bones are also removed. Set fish aside. If frozen spinach is used, defrost and boil quickly in water for 3 minutes. Drain, chill in cold water, drain again, and squeeze out. Saute onions and garlic in oil until light yellow, add spices and spinach. Cook until thoroughly hot and well mixed. Cool. Add cheese and fish.

Note: The flavor of Swiss cheese varies; the better the quality cheese used, the better the flavor will be.

#R 145

Smoked Whitefish and Chives

Yield: 40 pieces

16 oz	450 g	smoked whitefish, skin and bones removed
½ cup	0.11 l	chives, diced
8 oz	225 g	cream cheese

Flake whitefish. Combine chives with cream cheese, add whitefish.

Spinach Filling (vegetarian)   #R 146

Yield: Filling for 40 pieces

Use ingredients as in recipe #R 144, page 62, but eliminate the trout.

Vegetable Filling   #R 147

Yield: Filling for 65 pieces

3 cups	*0.70 l*	*firm zucchini, cut in dice*
1 cup	*0.23 l*	*tomato, diced, peeled,*
and		*seeded*
½ cup	*0.11 l*	*canned green, poblano*
		chili, peeled
1 cup	*0.23 l*	*cheddar cheese, shredded*
2 tbsp	*2 tbsp*	*masa harina*

Combine all ingredients in food processor. Do not puree, mixture should be coarse. Use in items that will be cooked or steamed.

Hot fillings for tartlets, brioche, and croustades

Cheese Curd   #R 148

Yield: Filling for 50

5	*5*	*egg yolks*
½ tsp	*½ tsp*	*white pepper, ground*
1 cup	*0.23 l*	*ale (beer)*
1 cup	*0.23 l*	*Parmesan cheese, grated*
8 oz	*225 g*	*brie cheese, soft, rind*
		removed

Combine egg yolks, pepper, and ale and stir over waterbath until thick. Add cheeses and stir over low heat until hot.

#R 149   # Curried Beef and Chutney Filling

Yield: 50 pieces

1 tbsp	1 tbsp	oil
1 tbsp	1 tbsp	curry powder
16 oz	450 g	ground beef
2 cups	0.46 l	mango chutney
		salt to taste

Put oil in heavy saucepan, add curry powder and saute 1 minute over low heat. Add ground beef, broken into pieces. Saute slowly, stirring frequently and breaking beef into small pieces. Cook until beef is done and crumbly. Drain off any excess fat. Put chutney in food processor and chop coarsely. Combine with cooked beef, add salt if desired.

#R 150   # Escargots and Spinach Filling

Yield: 48 pieces

20 oz	560 g	cello pack spinach (2 bags)
½ cup	0.11 l	onions, chopped
¼ tsp	¼ tsp	garlic, chopped
¼ cup	0.06 l	oil
1 cup	0.23 l	mild, cooked ham, chopped
1 tbsp	1 tbsp	Pernod
48	48	medium size escargots, canned
½ cup	0.11 l	fresh bread crumbs
½ cup	0.11 l	butter, melted

Wash spinach, place in pot, cover, and cook at high heat. There should be enough moisture clinging to the leaves to make the addition of water unnecessary. As soon as cooked, spread on baking sheet to cool. Chop coarsely. Saute onions and garlic in oil, add ham, chopped spinach, Pernod, and escargots. Season and cool mixture.

Note: When used in cream puffs keep mixture hot. When used in tartlets, fill with cool mixture, sprinkle with bread crumbs and butter, warm and brown in oven as needed.

Escargots with Herbs

#R 151

Yield: Filling for 48 pieces

2 cans	2 cans	escargots 4 oz (112 g) each, 24 count
2 tbsp	2 tbsp	shallots, chopped
¼ tsp	¼ tsp	garlic, chopped
1 tbsp	1 tbsp	oil
½ tsp	½ tsp	tarragon, chopped
1 cup	0.23 l	dry white wine
½ cup	0.11 l	ham, chopped
1 tsp	1 tsp	cornstarch
½ tbsp	½ tbsp	parsley, chopped
		salt and pepper to taste

Drain escargots and rinse. Saute shallots and garlic in oil, add tarragon, wine, and ham. Bring to boil and simmer 10 minutes. Moisten cornstarch with a little cold water and add to boiling mixture. Bring to boil, add snails and parsley. Season to taste.

Fennel (Anise) Puree

#R 152

Yield: 3 cups

2 lb	900 g	fresh fennel (about 3 bulbs)
1 cup	0.23 l	dry white wine
½ tsp	½ tsp	cardamon, ground
1 tsp	1 tsp	sugar
1 tbsp	1 tbsp	flour
		salt and pepper to taste

Clean bulbs, save some green leaves. Cut bulbs in chunks and chop in food processor into small, even pieces. Use pulse on/off. Put vegetable, wine, and spice in nonstick flat pot, cover and braise until vegetables are cooked but still crisp and most liquid is evaporated. Sprinkle with flour, bring to boil and cook until filling is thick. Add chopped leaves, season to taste.

#R 153

Finnan Haddie in Cream Sauce

Yield: 153

2 lb	900 g	Finnan Haddie
½ cup	0.23 l	milk
1	1	bay leaf
2 cups	0.46 l	heavy cream sauce
4	4	eggs, hard boiled
2 tbsp	2 tbsp	parsley, chopped

Cut Finnan Haddie in large dice and remove all bones. Cover with milk and water, add bay leaf, bring to boil, simmer until cooked. Cool in stock. Remove fish and flake. Add to hot cream sauce, add chopped eggs and parsley.

#R 154

Ham and Sherry

Yield: 50

2 cups	0.46 l	cooked ham, cut in small dice
1 cup	0.23 l	Amontillado sherry
2 cups	0.46 l	heavy cream
2 tsp	2 tsp	flour
6 tbsp	6 tbsp	chives, diced

Combine ham, heavy cream, and sherry, bring to a boil, stirring frequently until most of the liquid is reduced. Sprinkle with flour, stir well, add chives. The filling should be flavorful and not runny.

Note: The flavor of the dish is influenced by the salt content of the ham used. Most commercial ham is not too salty and works well.

Miso Filling for Tartlets and Vegetables   **#R 155**

Yield: Filling for 50

1 cup	0.23 l	Chu (golden miso)
1 cup	0.23 l	Mirin (Japanese sweet rice beer)
3 cups	0.70 l	fresh white bread crumbs

Combine all ingredients. Add warm water if necessary to make a paste which can be filled into tartlets.

Note: Miso is very salty and the bread is used as filler to reduce the salt content. Miso will not harden when heated. If it is used in a filling that will be baked or steamed, 3 egg whites should be added.

Mushrooms with Sherry   **#R 156**

Yield: Filling for 50

4 cups	0.92 l	white mushrooms, cut into small dice
4 oz	112 g	butter
2 oz	56 g	flour
1 cup	0.23 l	medium dry sherry
1 cup	0.23 l	heavy cream
		salt and pepper

Saute mushrooms in butter, sprinkle with flour, stir well. Add sherry wine, bring to boil, add cream and boil until mixture is thick and heavy.

#R 157   # White Mushroom Puree

Yield: 4 cups (0.92 l)

2 lb	900 g	white mushrooms
2 tbsp	2 tbsp	oil
¼ cup	0.06 l	chopped shallots
3 tbsp	3 tbsp	lemon juice
3 tbsp	3 tbsp	flour
1 cup	0.23 l	medium dry sherry
1 cup	0.23 l	light cream
		salt and pepper to taste

Wash mushrooms and drain well. Chop in food processor, with pulse on/off to make very small, evenly chopped pieces. Put oil in nonstick sauce pot, saute shallots until limp, add mushrooms and lemon juice. Cook over high heat until mushrooms are cooked and most liquid has evaporated. Sprinkle with flour, mix well. Add sherry and cream, bring to boil, and boil over high heat until mixture is thick so it can be spread on croustades or filled into tartlets. Season to taste.

#R 158   # Wild Mushroom Puree

Yield: 3 cups (0.70 l)

3 oz	85 g	dried wild mushrooms* (any kind)
1 lb	450 g	brown mushrooms
1 tbsp	1 tbsp	lemon juice
2 tbsp	2 tbsp	oil
½ cup	0.11 l	shallots, chopped
1 cup	0.23 l	fresh bread crumbs
3 tbsp	3 tbsp	flour
1 cup	0.23 l	dry white wine
		salt and pepper to taste

Soak dry mushrooms overnight. Bring to boil with soaking liquid and boil 10 minutes. Drain and save liquid. Wash fresh mushrooms, drain well. Chop cooked and fresh mushrooms in food processor, with pulse on/off to make very small, evenly chopped pieces. Put oil in nonstick sauce pot, saute shallots until limp, add mushrooms and lemon juice. Cook over high heat until mushrooms are cooked and most liquid has evaporated. Sprinkle with flour, mix well. Add white wine, mushroom stock,* and bread crumbs, bring to boil and boil over high heat until mixture is thick so it can be spread on croustades or filled into tartlets. Season to taste.

* Dried mushrooms can be sandy. Drain off stock carefully.

Red Pepper Coulis #R 159

Yield: 3 cups (0.70 l)

2 jars (14 oz each)	2 jars (400 g each)	red peppers, in water, peeled or 12 medium size red peppers
2 tbsp	2 tbsp	oil
1 tsp	1 tsp	garlic, chopped
2 tbsp	2 tbsp	capers
6	6	anchovy fillets
1 tsp	1 tsp	black pepper
		salt to taste

Drain canned peppers and puree in food processor with remaining ingredients.

Note: If fresh peppers are used, broil until black on all sides, place in bowl, and cover for steam to develop. When peppers have cooled they can be peeled and seeds removed. Peppers can also be peeled by deep-frying them. Red pepper puree can be used hot as a dip or cold as a spread.

Basic Risotto #R 160

Yield: 5 cups (1.15 l)

¼ cup	0.06 l	olive oil
2 cups	0.46 l	Arborio rice
½ cup	0.11 l	onions, chopped
6 cups	1.40 l	chicken stock
4 oz	112 g	butter, cold
1 cup	0.23 l	Parmesan cheese

Saute rice in oil, add chopped onions and saute 5 minutes longer. Add stock, stirring constantly as rice absorbs more moisture. The rice should be thick, but the kernels should still be firm to the bite. The cooking time is about 20 minutes. Just before service, add butter and cheese.

Note: Risotto will thicken while kept warm, and hot stock is needed to keep mixture at the right consistency.

#R 161

Salmon, Basil, and Mustard Filling

Yield: Filling for 50 pieces

20 oz	*560 g*	*salmon fillet, skin removed*
½ cup	*0.11 l*	*dry white wine*
2 tbsp	*2 tbsp*	*oil*
2 tbsp	*2 tbsp*	*flour*
1 cup	*0.23 l*	*light cream*
3 tbsp	*3 tbsp*	*prepared mustard*
3 tbsp	*3 tbsp*	*fresh basil leaves, chopped*
		pepper to taste

Make sure all bones are removed from salmon. Cut into 1 in. (25 mm) squares, add wine, cover, and poach over low heat until fish is cooked. Cool, drain off juices (save juices), and crumble fish. Cook oil and flour until light yellow, add cream and strained fish juices. Bring to boil, add salmon, mustard, and basil. Adjust flavor and consistency if necessary.

#R 162

Shrimp and Dill Filling

Yield: 2½ cup (0.58 l)

2 cups	*0.46 l*	*cooked, chopped shrimp*
½ cup	*0.11 l*	*mayonnaise*
2 tbsp	*2 tbsp*	*prepared mustard*
4 tbsp	*4 tbsp*	*fresh dill, chopped*
		cayenne pepper to taste

Combine ingredients and keep filling chilled. Use as needed and warm in oven.

Tapenade

#R 163

Yield: 4 cups (0.92 l)

24 oz	675 g	eggplants (3 large)
		salt
1½ cups	0.34 l	olive oil
1 tsp	1 tsp	garlic, crushed
½ cup	0.11 l	onions, chopped
1 tsp	1 tsp	fresh thyme, chopped
		juice of 2 lemons
1 cup	0.23 l	fresh white bread crumbs

Peel eggplant, cut in 1 in. (25 mm) slices, sprinkle with salt. Let stand 1 hour and squeeze out juices. Brush slices with oil and grill or oven roast until cooked. Put all items except bread crumbs and remaining oil in food processor and process pulse on/off to make puree. Add oil and bread crumbs in small amounts and proceed to smooth paste. The amount of oil and bread crumbs needed will vary depending on water content of eggplants. The paste should be spreadable.

Turkey Mole Filling

#R 164

Yield: 3 cups (0.70 l)

24 oz	675 g	turkey meat, ground
3 tbsp	3 tbsp	oil
½ cup	0.11 l	almonds, chopped
2 tbsp	2 tbsp	flour or masa harina
1 cup	0.23 l	water
2 tbsp	2 tbsp	mole powder
2 tbsp	2 tbsp	cilantro, chopped

Saute turkey meat with oil and almonds until brown and crumbled. Sprinkle with flour or masa, mix well. Add remaining ingredients, bring to boil. Adjust seasoning. Use hot in tartlets or in filo nests.

#R 165   Whitefish, Apple, and Caper Filling

Yield: Filling for 50 pieces

2 cups	0.46 l	apples, diced and peeled
½ cup	0.11 l	balsamic vinegar
32 oz	900 g	smoked whitefish, all skin and bones removed
¼ cup	0.06 l	capers
1 tsp	1 tsp	cayenne pepper

Combine apples with vinegar and simmer until soft. Chill. Break whitefish into small pieces and combine with apples, capers, and cayenne pepper.

Dips, marinades, relishes, and sauces

#R 166   Asparagus Dip

Yield: 5 cups (1.15 l)

4 lb	1.80 kg	green asparagus
2 tbsp	2 tbsp	cornstarch
		salt and pepper

Peel asparagus and cut into fine slices to cut the fibers.* Cover with water, bring to boil and boil until tender. Dilute cornstarch with cold water, add to vegetable to thicken. Chill/cool vegetable as quickly as possible to preserve green color and vitamins. Puree in food processor, season to taste.

* Do not use tough stalk ends.

Green Mint Puree

#R 167

Yield: 4 cups (0.92 l)

2 cups	0.46 l	apple juice
4 cups	0.92 l	mint leaves, well washed and chopped
1 tsp	1 tsp	unflavored gelatin
1 tbsp	1 tbsp	cornstarch
2 oz	56 g	green crème de menthe
2 tbsp	2 tbsp	mint jelly
1 cup	0.23 l	applesauce, unsweetened

Combine apple juice and mint leaves. Bring to boil and let steep at about 180°F/80°C for 2 hours. Sprinkle gelatin over apple/mint liquid. Bring to boil again. Mix cornstarch with 2 tbsp cold water and add slurry to boiling liquid. Cool. Add remaining ingredients. Process in food processor to make smooth puree. Serve cold.

Green Lime Dip

#R 168

Yield: 6 cups (1.40 l)

12	12	limes
2 cups	0.46 l	ripe mango chunks
1 cup	0.23 l	green mango chunks
2 tbsp	2 tbsp	amchoor powder
¼ cup	0.11 l	ginger, chopped
1 cup	0.23 l	sugar
1 tsp	1 tsp	cayenne pepper

Cut limes in half; remove seeds. Put in food processor with 1 cup (0.23 l) cold water, process with pulse on/off until chopped. Add other ingredients and process until well mixed to a coarse puree. Refrigerate for one week before use. Dilute if necessary with water.

#R 169 ## Lemon Chutney

Yield: 3 cups (0.70 l)

12	12	large lemons
1 cup	0.23 l	apples, chopped
1 cup	0.23 l	brown sugar
¼ tsp	¼ tsp	cardamom
¼ tsp	¼ tsp	anise, ground
⅛ tsp	⅛ tsp	cayenne pepper
½ tbsp	½ tbsp	lemongrass, chopped

Peel lemons with vegetable peeler and chop peels in food processor. Remove white skin from peeled lemons and discard. Cut lemons in small dice, discard seeds but save juice. Combine lemons, juice, peels, sugar, and apples in nonstick pot and bring to boil. Add spices and cook until thick.

#R 170 ## Pesto

Yield: 7 cups (1.60 l)

8 cups	1.84 l	basil leaves
½ cup	0.11 l	garlic, chopped
2 cups	0.46 l	pine nuts
3 cups	0.70 l	Parmesan cheese
2 cups	0.46 l	olive oil

Process in food processor to smooth puree.

Note: Commercially prepared frozen pesto is available. The supply and price of basil leaves depends on season.

Pickled Ginger Dip

#R 171

Yield: 8 cups (1.85 l)

1 lb	450 g	*sweet potatoes, cooked*
1 cup	0.23 l	*carrots, grated*
1 cup	0.23 l	*seedless raisins*
1 cup	0.23 l	*apples, peeled and diced*
1 cup	0.23 l	*white vinegar*
1 cup	0.23 l	*water*
1 cup	0.23 l	*ginger, peeled and sliced*
½ cup	0.11 l	*sugar*
½ tsp	½ tsp	*cayenne pepper*

Cube sweet potatoes. Combine all ingredients, bring to boil, cover and braise 30 minutes. Cool and puree.

Roast Corn Relish

#R 172

Yield: 8 cups (1.85 l)

10 ears	10 ears	*sweet corn*
4	4	*large red peppers*
2	2	*large green peppers*
2 tbsp	2 tbsp	*brown sugar*
2 cups	0.46 l	*cider vinegar*
1 cup	0.23 l	*onions, chopped*
1 tbsp	1 tbsp	*fresh ginger*
1 tsp	1 tsp	*butcher ground pepper*
		salt to taste

Husk corn and place on top of stove to brown. Turn to brown evenly. Cool and shuck. Remove seeds from peppers and dice. Bring sugar and vinegar to boil, add corn kernels, cover and cook 5 minutes. Add onions, diced peppers, ginger, and seasoning. Bring to boil once more. Cool and marinate at least 24 hours.

#R 173 ## Roasted Tomato Salsa

Yield: 7 cups (1.60 l)

2 lb	900 g	Italian plum tomatoes
1 cup	0.23 l	olive oil
1 tbsp	1 tbsp	garlic, chopped
1 cup	0.23 l	onions, chopped
1 cup	0.23 l	tomatoes, fine dice
1 cup	0.23 l	green onions (scallions), diced
1 cup	0.23 l	cilantro leaves, chopped
1 tbsp	1 tbsp	Jalapeño pepper, chopped
1 tsp	1 tsp	oregano, chopped
2 tbsp	2 tbsp	lime juice
2 tbsp	2 tbsp	salt

Rub tomatoes with oil, spread in roasting pan, and put under the broiler* until the tomato skin starts to brown and blister. Turn tomatoes frequently to roast evenly. When tomatoes are brown add garlic and onions. Cook in oven until pulp is soft. Cool, puree in food processor and strain through a coarse china cap. Add remaining ingredients, including remaining oil. Refrigerate 1 day before use. Adjust seasoning if necessary.

* If broiler is not available, a very hot oven can be used. The tomatoes can also be split and placed, cut side down on the stove top to brown.

#R 174 ## Salsa

Yield: 7 cups (1.60 l)

1 cup	0.23 l	cilantro leaves, chopped
1 cup	0.23 l	onions, chopped
2 cups	0.46 l	tomatoes, fine dice
1 cup	0.23 l	cucumbers, peeled, seeded, and diced
1 tbsp	1 tbsp	garlic, chopped
2 tbsp	2 tbsp	ginger, chopped
1 tsp	1 tsp	Jalapeño pepper, chopped
2 tbsp	2 tbsp	lime juice
2 tbsp	2 tbsp	salt
1 cup	0.23 l	olive oil

Combine all ingredients and refrigerate for 2 days.

Note: Make sure cilantro leaves are well washed before they are chopped. All ingredients could be chopped together in the food processor.

Taramasalata Dip

Yield: 6 cups (1.40 l)

16 oz	225 g	salted carp roe (available in Greek stores)
1 cup	0.23 l	tajimi paste
		juice of 2 lemons
2 cups	0.46 l	oil
3 cups	0.70 l	white bread, crust removed and diced
		ground white pepper to taste

Combine roe, tajimi paste, and lemon juice in food processor. Blend. Add oil and bread in small increments to make a smooth paste. The amount of oil and bread needed depends on the saltiness of the carp roe.

Tomatillo Dip

Yield: 6 cups (1.40 l)

16 oz	450 g	tomatillos
1 cup	0.23 l	red wine vinegar
16 oz	450 g	cucumbers
16 oz	450 g	tomatoes
8 oz	225 g	red (Bermuda) onions, peeled
1 tbsp	1 tbsp	garlic, chopped
1 tbsp	1 tbsp	fresh chili pepper, chopped
1 cup	0.23 l	oil
		salt to taste

Remove husks from tomatillos, wash and cut in large cubes. Add vinegar and bring to boil. Chill. Peel tomatoes and cucumbers, remove seeds. Puree in food processor tomatillos, cucumbers, and tomatoes. Add garlic, chili peppers, and oil. Season to taste. Marinate at least 24 hours before use.

#R 177 Onion Confit

Yield: 6 cups (1.40 l)

¼ cup	0.06 l	olive oil
1 tbsp	1 tbsp	garlic, chopped
2 tbsp	2 tbsp	ginger, chopped
24 oz	670 g	red onions, chopped
12 oz	330 g	green apples, diced and peeled
8 oz	225 g	dried apricots, diced
1	1	peel of orange, chopped
2	2	peel of lemons, chopped
¾ cup	0.17 l	cider vinegar
¼ tsp	¼ tsp	allspice
¼ tsp	¼ tsp	cloves, ground
¼ tsp	¼ tsp	cayenne pepper
¼ cup	0.06 l	sugar
1 cup	0.23 l	water

Saute garlic and ginger in olive oil until light brown. Add all other ingredients, stir well, cover, and simmer over slow heat about one hour. Refrigerate for two days.

#R 178 Grave Lax Seasoning Mix

Yield: Seasoning for 5 lb (1.4 kg) salmon fillet

¼ cup	0.06 l	coriander seeds, crushed
¾ cup	0.17 l	salt
1½ cup	0.34 l	sugar
¼ cup	0.06 l	black pepper, crushed
2 bunches	2 bunches	dill

Dry toast coriander seeds in frying pan, do not brown. Crush and mix with sugar, salt, and pepper. Wash dill and chop coarsely. Salmon fillet should be on the skin and all bones should be removed. Rub salmon generously with spice mixture and sprinkle with dill. Place in stainless steel pan, skin down, cover, and refrigerate. Turn salmon each day. Curing should take about 48 hours.

Dry Smoke Mix

#R 179

Yield: Seasoning for 10 lb (2.8 kg) salmon fillet

16 oz	450 g	salt
8 oz	225 g	brown sugar
1 tbsp	1 tbsp	coriander, ground
1 tbsp	1 tbsp	white pepper, ground
1 tbsp	1 tbsp	allspice, ground

Combine ingredients and rub fish fillets on both sides. Marinate about 6 hours. Smoke until fish is firm.

Note: Suitable for smoking are fatty fish varieties such as mackerel, trout, sturgeon, eel, and herring.

chapter **5**

COLD CANAPES

The cold canapes displays in this section are arranged alphabetically by occasion and numbered from #C 101 to #C 124. The individual cold canapes begin with number #C 130. The recipes of the components used in the preparation of these canapes are listed alphabetically in Chapter 4, Basic Recipes, and begin with #RC 50.

Cold canapes lend themselves to lavish or whimsical decorations. They can be made ahead within reason, or the components can be made ahead and assembled just before service.

The following canapes are elegant examples how beautiful food can look when the natural colors are skillfully combined and food products are artistically displayed, particularly when presented on beautiful platters as shown here. In some cases, the shape, color, and size of the serving trays sets the mood for a party.

The canapes in this chapter should stimulate the imagination of the reader and are not meant to be copied exactly.

Canapes by Themes

#C 101 Antipasto Display

On the left side is a bouquet of enoki mushrooms in an artichoke flower. The cold cuts consist of sliced daikon radish, salami, cheese, and smoked turkey. Other ingredients are roasted green and red pepper, fried fish cake, daikon slices, olives, red radishes, chives, red pepper flowers, dill gerkhins, eggplant, yellow squash, and alfalfa sprouts.

The squash flowers contain cocktail sauce and Dijon mustard mayonnaise. Additional sauce will be served on the side.

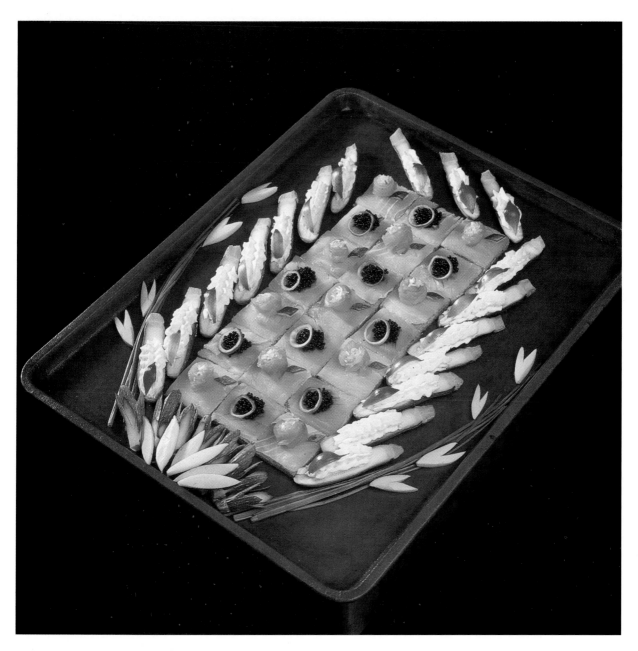

Birthday Canapes

#C 102

Smoked sturgeon canapes on cocktail rye bread. The canapes are garnished alternately with smoked salmon roses and with caviar. Around the platter are small zucchini filled with cream cheese. Vegetable flowers are made with yellow squash and chives.

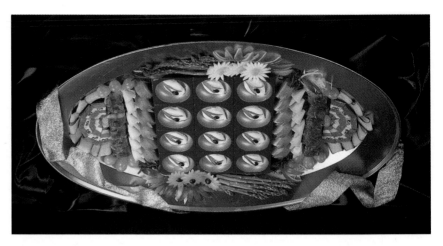

#C 103

Buffet Party

The center is dominated by small slices of chicken breast and paté, covered with a gelatin stiffened sour cream sauce. Next is a fish terrine, covered with smoked salmon slices. The canapes are all on pumpernickel bread. They consist of provolone cheese and baby corn, smoked mackerel, smoked sturgeon, and smoked salmon. Various vegetables are used as decorations.

#C 103

Christmas Canapes

This seafood display emphasized the color red. The lobster tails are sliced; the center bowl is filled with crab meat and is surrounded by shrimp. The bowl at the bottom is filled with shucked baby clams surrounded by radicchio lettuce. Poached fish is placed around the bowl. Stuffed endives, chive flowers, alfalfa sprouts, and various vegetables are used as garnish. The sauce dishes contain cocktail sauce and mustard mayonnaise.

Cocktail for Two #C 105

Two identical plates emphasize the theme. Each plate consists of skewers of sausage, cheese, fig half, and a ball of Bartlett pear. Next to the skewers are two pieces of smoked salmon and cucumber slices tightly rolled together and tied with a leek string. The canapes are made with pepperoni and cheese squares. The red sticks are boiled rhubarb filled with cream cheese. Vegetable flowers complement the plates.

#C 106   Crudité

An effective arrangement. Starting in the center and going clockwise are yellow peppers and avocado balls; sliced avocado; avocado filled with horseradish mustard dip; endives, snow peas and green peppers; asparagus and yellow peppers; green pepper petals and yellow pepper; and red cabbage with asparagus tid bits.

Diet Canapes

#C 107

The display is all vegetarian and uses sushi rice, recipe #R 126, page 53. The toppings are, from right to left: carrot flower and thyme sprig, yellow pepper flower, daikon radish flower and red pepper, radish rose filled with egg yolk. The garnish is long chives and cranberries.

Note: Sushi rice is traditionally served lukewarm. The canapes should be assembled at the last moment, which is not difficult if all components are ready.

#C 108   Easter

The color scheme is yellow. The display is more artistic than practical and is to stimulate the imagination. Starting at the bottom triangle and moving clockwise: prosciutto roses on pumpernickel bread; foie gras ball rolled in chopped egg whites, egg yolks and truffles on bay leaf skewers; smoked turkey breast cones on walnut rye bread; zucchini roses filled with mango shrimp salad; cured mozzarella and ham; red cabbage leaves with poached scallops, dab of horseradish mustard, and red caviar.

Garnish is made of blanched leek leaves and yellow squash.

Note: Fresh bay leaves still on the stems are available from specialty produce purveyors.

Engagement Canapes (Buffet Display)   **#C 109**

Starting at the right side next to the wine glasses: strawberries with
cream cheese; marinated baby beets on pumpernickel garnished with fresh
rosemary; cauliflower and fresh mozzarella; fresh apricot halves; red radish
flowers; yellow teardrop tomatoes filled with herb cream cheese; green
tomatoes filled with sun-dried tomatoes, basil, and olives; red tomatoes
with crabmeat salad.

In the foreground are marinated stuffed tiny potatoes. Sliced lotus roots,
leaves, chives, and vegetables are used as garnish.

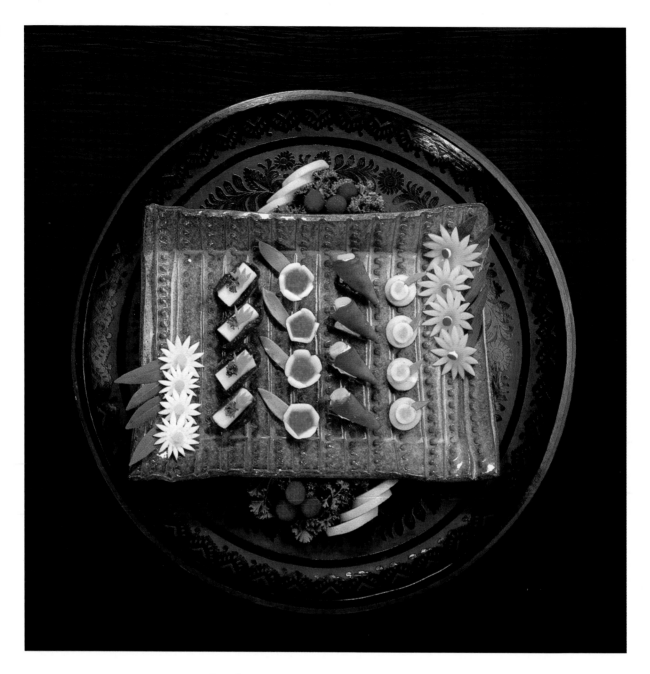

#C 110   Father's Day

Starting at the right side, next to the yellow squash flowers: cucumber circles topped with scallop; sliced dried beef on pumpernickel bread with cream cheese and avocado; squash tulip filled with red caviar (the leaves are fresh bay leaves); Polly-o string cheese on pumpernickel bread garnished with sun-dried tomatoes.

The flowers on the left side are made with turnips.

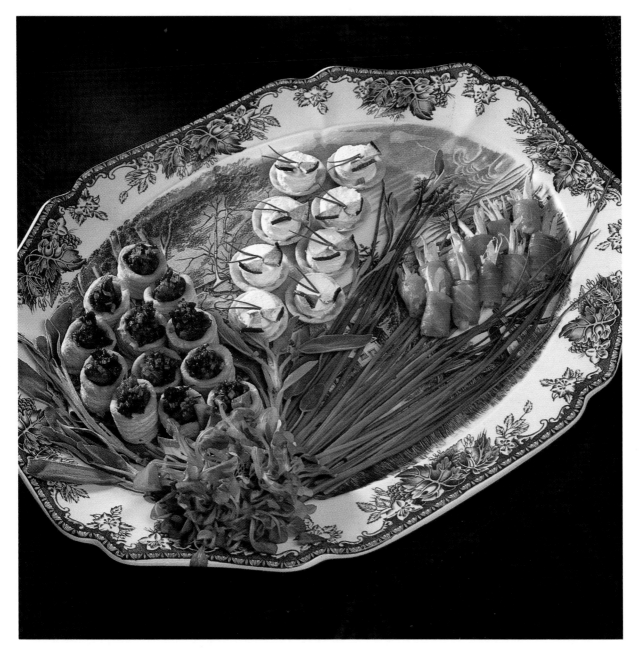

Garden Look Canapes

#C 111

Starting at the left side: small patty shells filled with a tasty salad of smoked oysters, marinated sun-dried tomatoes, spices and chives; in the center are tartlets with goat cheese garnished with dried apple slices; on the right side are bundles of smoked salmon wrapped around endive. Mache (Lamb lettuce), long chives and sage leaves emphasize the garden feeling.

#C 112 Golden Anniversary

This colorful display is stunning yet simple. The center consists of quail eggs filled with red caviar. The leaves are snow peas and cream cheese. Outside the platter are filled cherry tomatoes topped with Oriental egg omelette, recipe #RC 52, on page 40.

Lobster Sunburst

#C 113

The outside petals are endive leaves filled with tuna tartare recipe #RC 57, page 42. The next circle consists of lobster medallions on round toast, horseradish mayonnaise garnished with sliced lobster claws.

The center consists of small tartlets filled with black caviar. The sunflowers are made with yellow squash petals and shiitake mushrooms.

#C 114   Mother's Day Canapes

Starting at the left side: silver cups filled with carrot flowers and enoki mushrooms; stuffed grape leaves filled with sushi rice, recipe #R 126, page 53; cucumber slices with pimento spread, recipe #RC 53, page 40; smoked salmon, seaweed and mushrooms; smoked trout spread, recipe #RC 56 page 42, wrapped in moo-shu shells.

Spoons filled with lump fish caviar and salmon spread recipe #RC 54, page 41.

New Year

#C 115

This display is presented on a Chinese platter and garnished with red flowers signifying luck.

Starting at the bottom row; the canapes are: mousse of foie gras on pumpernickel with mango; smoked salmon with cream cheese on pumpernickel bread, garnished with dill and red caviar; fish mousse, recipe #R 136, page 58, made with salmon—the red section—and made with white fish and spinach puree; endive leaves, filled with pickled red cabbage, cucumbers, radishes, and cooked eggplants, seasoned with vinegar, sugar, salt, and pepper.

#C 116 Oriental Canapes

Four identical china dishes on a twig mat. Starting at the right-hand corner: radish flower with chopped egg yolk; shrimp on slice of fish terrine; bundle of enoki mushrooms rolled in roasted seaweed; egg omelette cut in tulip shape; cucumber cups filled with red smelt caviar.

Picture Frame

#C 117

The smoked salmon canapes on walnut/rye bread are garnished with simple flowers. The stems are made with blanched leeks, the flowers with yellow squash and truffles.

#C 118 Royal Canapes

The name refers to the "royal" color.

Starting at the right, next to the flower: vegetable terrine, recipe #RC 58, page 143 (the center is heart of palm and carrot puree); next are purple potatoes filled with cream cheese on sesame leaves; chicken pieces are on the left. The flower is made with red onions.

Seafood Display

#C 119

Starting with the spoons: they are filled with egg yolk mayonnaise spread and topped with carp roe; rice crackers, cream cheese, anchovy fillets and thyme; celery with Boursin cheese, papaya garnish, eggplant tulips (quickly cooked in lemon water) filled with marinated Brussels sprouts, garnished with radish; shucked oyster, cocktail sauce, horseradish, and parsley.

#C 120   Silver Anniversary

Top level: smoked salmon tartare, recipe #RC 55 page 41, surrounded by lemon peel.

Middle level: smoked sliced beef. The center filling is made with cooked egg yolk, horseradish, mustard, mayonnaise. The strings are cooked leeks.

Bottom level: avocado quarters with strawberry cream cheese. The flowers are made of white turnips.

Summer Canapes

#C 121

The whimsical dishes are fun. The food items are simple: quail eggs whole and filled with black or red caviar. Red onion slivers, capers, and sliced lemon are the garnish.

#C 122   Thanksgiving

Five oval platters presented on a flat basket. Starting at the bottom and going counterclockwise: mozzarella, sun-dried tomatoes, basil, snow peas; boiled eggs and red caviar; two color fish mousse, recipe #R 136 page 58, the red section made with salmon and the white part made with a white fish and colored with spinach puree; sardines on thin crisp bread with chopped egg yolks and dill; smoked salmon spread, recipe #RC 54 page 41, rolled in seaweed, and chilled.

Vegetable Flowers

#C 123

The colorful and edible flowers can be easily identified. Besides blue cheese, mayonnaise, and cocktail sauce, other suitable dipping sauces are: asparagus dip recipe #R 166 page 72, red pepper coulis, recipe #R 159, page 69, roast corn relish recipe #R 172, page 75, roasted tomato salsa recipe #R 173, page 76, salsa recipe #R 174, page 76, taramasalata dip recipe #R 175 page 77, tomatillo dip recipe #R 176, page 77.

#C 124   Wedding Canapes

The Calla lilies in the foreground are made with thin turnip slices and baby corn. Starting on the left side are: yellow pepper wedges with crab-meat, shrimp and lobster salad; red pepper wedges, pickled herring, Japanese horseradish (wasabe), baby corn slice; canned litchi, smoked duckling, radicchio leaves; sliced raw beef (carpaccio) on daikon slice, dill gherkins. Chive flowers.

Individual Canapes

The tray holds three individual canapes.

Top row: baby red potatoes filled with caviar; Middle row: lobster salad, capers, shiitake mushroom on toast; Bottom row: skewers with smoked mussels and sun-dried tomatoes. The skewers are decorated with zucchini. On the bottom are dried apple slices.

#C 125 Salmon dill terrine, green hot sauce.

#C 126 Tri-colored pasta, marinated with olive oil, pesto, and vinegar, purple basil leaves.

#C 127 Vegetable terrine, recipe #RC 58, page 43, basil leaves and green pepper.

#C 128 Rolled pastrami, dill gherkins, rosemary, and red pepper.

#C 129 Marinated eggplant slices (use recipe #RC 51, page 39, for marinated eggplant spread but do not puree), chives, pink peppercorns.

#C 130 Fresh kumquats, blanched, halved, and filled with paté, mint leaves.

#C 131 Goat cheese with star fruit (carambola).

#C 132 Passion fruit halves, salami cones with cocktail onions.

#C 133 Radish rose filled with tartare steak, recipe #H 237, page 192, (do not grill), and wasabe.

#C 134 Marinated shiitake mushrooms stuffed with a salad of mushrooms, sun-dried tomatoes, thyme, and beets.

#C 135 Pastrami slices rolled around asparagus. The garnish consists of asparagus slices and red cabbage leaves.

#C 136 House paté with mango ball and small truffle slice on top of toast.

#C 137 Turkey breast cones arranged as flower with fresh bay leaves, mango balls, and thyme.

#C 138 Poached salmon, mustard with green peppers, radish flower.

#C 139 Smoked chicken breast on pumpernickel.

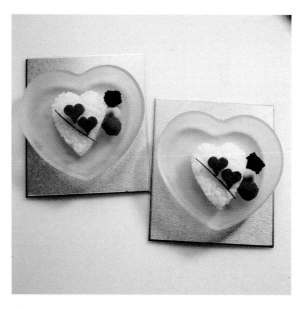

#C 140 Heart shaped sushi rice, beet hearts, beet horseradish, black lump fish caviar.

#C 141 Salmon mousse spread, recipe #RC 54, page 41, in small potato, lump fish caviar, and vegetable flower decorations.

#C 142 Pattypan and zucchini squash filled with smoked trout spread, recipe #RC 56, page 42 and liver mousse.

#C 143 Seaweed (nori) cones filled with sushi rice, pickled burdock, and wasabe.

#C 144 Little neck clams, hot sauce, chives, red pepper, and lemon slices.

#C 145   Four carrot tulips filled with green and yellow vegetable terrine and cut in half, recipe #RC 58, page 43.

#C 146   Smoked chicken breast on pumpernickel bread, beet horse radish, purple basil leaves.

#C 147   Star fruit and goat cheese and shredded coconut "sandwich."

#C 148   Miniature toast with black caviar.

#C 149 Yukon gold potatoes filled with shredded seaweed seasoned with mirin and sesame oil.

#C 150 Kiwi slices on pumpernickel bread topped with liver mousse.

#C 151 Goat cheese on red pepper leaves garnished with mango balls and fresh bay leaves.

#C 152 Crepes filled with smoked trout spread, recipe #RC 56, page 42, on rice crackers, lump fish caviar garnish.

#C 153 Ham rolls filled with cream cheese and chives, rosemary and radish garnish, red pepper jelly on the side.

#C 154 Liver mousse (canned and creamed), truffle slice, chives on toast squares.

chapter 6

HOT HORS D'OEUVRES

Items in this sections are arranged alphabetically and are numbered with a prefix H (hot), beginning with recipe #H 101.

Baked Items

Bacon Rolls with Yeast   #H 101

Yield: 100 pieces

16 oz	*450 g*	*bacon*
1 pkg	*1 pkg*	*yeast*
1 tsp	*1 tsp*	*sugar*
1¼ cup	*0.29 l*	*milk*
16 oz	*450 g*	*flour*
1 tsp	*1 tsp*	*salt*
1 tsp	*1 tsp*	*red pepper*

Cook bacon until crisp. Drain fat and reserve ¼ cup (0.06 l). Crumble or chop bacon. Combine yeast with sugar and lukewarm milk. When yeast has dissolved, add 2 cups flour, spices, and bacon fat. Mix in food processor to smooth dough. Put dough on pastry board and work in remaining flour and bacon bits. Cover and let proof, punch down, and proof again. Scale ¼ oz (7 g) balls, proof again, egg wash, and bake at 400°F/200°C.

Biscuits

Miniature biscuits, about 1½ in. (37 mm) across and not higher than ½ in. (12 mm) are easy to make and are very user friendly. They can be popped right in the mouth without having to contend with crumbs and plates.

Biscuits can be frozen and baked on site at the last minute. It is important that the biscuits are well seasoned, crumbly but not dry.

Biscuits can be made from mix or from scratch. Small biscuits can be split and filled with a dab of filling, such as cheese curd, recipe #R 148, page 63, onion confit, recipe #R 177, page 78, or with sliced meat, such as Virginia ham.

Biscuits can also be flavored with tumeric, which will make them yellow, or with mixed herbs and flecks of hot red pepper.

The basic baking powder biscuits recipe #R 106 is on page 44.

Following are numerous biscuit variations.

#H 102   ## Bacon Biscuits

Yield: 50

24 oz	670 g	bacon
1 tsp	1 tsp	butcher ground pepper
		biscuit dough in recipe #R 106, page 44

Cook bacon until very crisp. Drain fat, cool bacon. Chop into fine crumbly pieces. Add bacon and pepper to biscuit dough. Chill. Roll ½ in. (12 mm) thick, cut into 1½ in. (37 mm) rounds or other bite-size shapes. Bake at 400°F/200°C.

Brie Cheese Biscuits

Yield: 100 pieces

16 oz	450 g	soft brie cheese
18 oz	500 g	cake flour
2 tbsp	2 tbsp	baking powder
6 oz	170 g	butter or margarine
4	4	egg yolks
1 tsp	1 tsp	nutmeg
		pinch of cayenne pepper
¾ cup	0.17 l	buttermilk

Brie cheese must be ripe and runny, but not smelling of ammoniac. Remove and discard rind; there should be about 12 oz (340 g) of cheese left after cleaning. Make dough on pastry board, add more flour if dough is very soft. Refrigerate dough. Roll ¼ in. (7 mm) thick, cut into rounds or triangles, egg wash and bake. Biscuits can be sprinkled with sesame seeds.

Cheddar Biscuits

#H 104

Yield: 70 pieces

12 oz	335 g	cake flour
4 oz	112 g	butter or margarine
1 tbsp	1 tbsp	baking powder
8 oz	225 g	sharp cheddar cheese, grated fine
1 tsp	1 tsp	paprika
½ cup	0.11 l	buttermilk

Combine all ingredients on pastry board to form a pliable dough. A little cold water might be needed if cheese is very dry. Let rest in refrigerator. Roll ¼ in. (7 mm) thick, cut into squares or rounds, bake at 375°F/180°C.

Silver platter with chili biscuits recipe #H 105, this page, and biscuits flavored with other spices.

#H 105 Chili Biscuits

Yield: 100 pieces

½ cup	*0.11 l*	*chili powder*
		biscuit dough recipe
		#R 106, page 44

Add chili powder to biscuit dough. Chill. Roll ½ in. (13 mm) thick, cut into 1½ in. (37 mm) rounds or other bite-size shapes. Bake at 400°F/200°C.

#H 106 Dill and Ham Biscuits

Yield: 100 pieces

		basic biscuit dough recipe
		#R 106, page 44
2 cups	*0.46 l*	*ham, cooked and chopped*
1 cup	*0.23 l*	*dill, chopped*
1 tsp	*1 tsp*	*cumin*

Combine above ingredients.

Hazelnut Biscuits

#H 107

Yield: 70 pieces

16 oz	450 g	soft (cake) flour
2 tbsp	2 tbsp	baking powder
1 tsp	1 tsp	salt
4 oz	112 g	butter
2	2	eggs
1 cup	0.23 l	buttermilk
1 cup	0.23 l	hazelnuts, chopped

Combine ingredients, handle dough as above and bake at 400°F/200°C about 20 minutes.

Herb Biscuits

#H 108

Yield: 100 pieces

		basic biscuit dough recipe #R 106, page 44
2 cups	0.46 l	fresh herbs, chopped

Combine ingredients, handle dough as above and bake at 400°F/200°C about 20 minutes.

Note: Make sure that herbs are well washed before they are chopped. Many herbs are very potent and care must be taken not to overpower the mix. At least 50 percent of the herb mixture should be parsley. Some fresh spinach can also be added for additional color.

Mozzarella Cheese Biscuits

#H 109

Yield: 100 pieces

2 cups	0.46 l	mozzarella cheese, shredded basic biscuit dough recipe #R 106, page 118

Combine ingredients, handle dough as above and bake at 400°F/200°C about 20 minutes.

#H 110

Parmesan Cheese Biscuits

Yield: 100 pieces

2 cups	0.46 l	*Parmesan cheese, grated*
		basic biscuit dough recipe
		#R 106, page 44

Combine ingredients, handle dough as above and bake at 400°F/200°C about 20 minutes.

Note: Other grating cheeses can also be used.

#H 111

Poppy Seed Biscuits

Yield: 100 pieces

2 cups	0.46 l	*poppy seeds*
1 tsp	1 tsp	*cinnamon, ground*
		basic biscuit dough recipe
		#R 106, page 44

Combine ingredients, handle dough as above, and bake at 400°F/200°C about 20 minutes.

Brioche

Although brioche is considered a breakfast pastry, it can be made with just little sugar and flavored with herbs and spices or stuffed. Brioche is traditionally baked in small molds garnished with a " hat" on top. For hors d'oeuvres, it can be advantageous to bake the dough in strips about 1 in. (25 mm) wide and ¼ in. (7 mm) thick. These strips can be covered with different fillings and are cut after baking into bite-size morsels. We call these strips brioche breads.

See directions for making brioche, recipes #HT 100 brioche on page 28.

Curry and Nuts Brioche   #H 112

Yield: 150 pieces

		brioche dough recipe #HT 100, page 28
4 tbsp	4 tbsp	curry powder
4 tbsp	4 tbsp	masala paste
2 cup	0.46 l	nuts (any kind), chopped

Add above ingredients when flour is added in recipe #HT 100.

Escargots Brioche   #H 113

Fill baked brioche with escargots, recipes #R 151 or #R 152, page 65.

Herb and Mozzarella Brioche Bread   #H 114

Yield: 150 pieces

1 cup	0.23 l	herbs, chopped
		brioche dough recipe #HT 100, page 28
		egg wash
24 oz	670 g	mozzarella cheese, shredded

Add chopped herbs to brioche dough according to taste. The herb mixture should not be too strong; about 50 percent should be parsley. A small amount of cooked pureed spinach will add additional color. Roll brioche dough into strips, about 1 in. (25 mm) wide and ¼ in. (7 mm) thick. Brush with egg wash and cover generously with cheese. Proof and bake at 400°F/200°C. Cut into bite-size slivers.

Basket of assorted mini brioche including mint brioche recipe #H 115, this page, curry and nuts brioche #H 112, page 121, and plain brioche recipe #HT 100, page 28.

#H 115

Mint Brioche

Yield: 150 pieces

		brioche dough recipe #HT 100, page 28
2 tbsp	2 tbsp	white crème de menthe liquor
10 tbsp	10 tbsp	fresh mint, chopped

Add liquor when flour is added in recipe #HT 100; add mint when dough is shaped.

On the board are five varieties of brioche bread. Starting at the right hand corner: mushrooms and pesto brioche bread, recipe #H 116, this page; tomatoes, anchovy, and thyme brioche bread recipe #H 124, page 126; brioche bread sprinkled with mozzarella cheese: Smoked salmon and rosemary brioche bread #H 122, page 125; poultry mousse brioche bread #H 117, page 124.

Mushrooms and Pesto Brioche Bread　　　　**#H 116**

Making brioche bread is more efficient than making individual brioche.

Yield: 150 pieces

> brioche dough recipe #HT 100, page 28
> prepared pesto recipe #R 170, page 74
> egg wash
> fresh or canned mushrooms

Roll brioche dough into strips, about 1 in. (25 mm) wide and ¼ in. (7 mm) thick. Brush with egg wash and then with pesto. Cover generously with sliced mushrooms. Brush with pesto again, proof, and bake at 400°F/200°C. Cut into bite-size slivers.

#H 117

Poultry Mousse Brioche Bread

Yield: 150 pieces

> *brioche dough recipe #HT 100, page 28*
> *poultry mousse recipe #R 140, page 60*
> *herbs, chopped*
> *egg wash*

Roll brioche dough into strips, about 1 in. (25 mm) wide and ¼ in. (7 mm) thick. Blend poultry mousse with herbs according to taste. Use pastry bag to pipe poultry mousse on dough. Brush with egg wash, proof, and bake at 400°F/200°C. Cut into bite-size slivers (see photo on page 123).

#H 118

Roquefort Cheese Brioche

Yield: 50

50 l	50 l	*brioche, not baked*
16 oz	450 g	*Roquefort cheese*

Prepare brioche. Before putting "hat" on top, make small hole in center and fill with crumbled cheese. Cover hole with hat and bake.

#H 119

Saffron Brioche

Yield: 150 pieces

1 tsp	1 tsp	*saffron, crushed or crumbled*
		brioche dough recipe
		#HT 100, page 28

Bring ½ cup hot water to boil, add saffron. Remove from heat and let steep until lukewarm. Use saffron flavored water in dough preparation.

Note: Saffron will not dissolve and some pieces will remain visible in dough. Saffron is very expensive. A much less expensive substitute is Ajiote, available in South American grocery stores. The black seeds must be cooked in a little oil to dissolve the color and flavor. Discard the seeds and use the oil when making the dough. Adjust the fat quantity in the recipe accordingly.

Sherry Mushrooms Brioche #H 120

Fill baked brioche with sherry mushrooms, recipe #R 156, page 67.

Shrimp in Dill Brioche #H 121

Fill baked brioche with shrimp in dill, recipe #R 162, page 70.

Smoked Salmon and Rosemary Brioche Bread #H 122

Yield: 150 pieces

> *fresh rosemary*
> *olive oil*
> *brioche dough recipe #HT 100, page 28*
> *egg wash*
> *smoked salmon*

Break rosemary into small clusters and soak in olive oil overnight. Roll brioche dough into strips, about 1 in. (25 mm) wide and ¼ in. (7 mm) thick. Egg wash and cover with smoked salmon slices. Arrange rosemary on top. Brush with same olive oil rosemary was soaked in. Proof and bake at 380°F/180°C. Cut into bite-size slivers (see photo on page 123).

Thyme Brioche #H 123

Yield: 150 pieces

		brioche dough recipe #HT 100, page 28
8 *tbsp*	8 *tbsp*	*fresh thyme, chopped (or 5 tbsp dried thyme)*
6 *tbsp*	6 *tbsp*	*Italian parsley, chopped*

Add herbs to brioche dough when dough is worked on the table. Follow basic recipe instructions for shaping, proofing, and baking brioche.

#H 124

Tomato, Anchovy and Thyme Brioche Bread

Yield: 150 pieces

fresh thyme
olive oil
brioche dough recipe #HT 100, page 28
egg wash
Italian plum tomatoes
anchovy fillets

Break thyme into small clusters and soak in olive oil overnight. Roll brioche dough into strips, about 1 in. (25 mm) wide and ¼ in. (7 mm) thick. Egg wash and cover with sliced tomatoes. Put anchovy fillets on top of tomatoes and arrange thyme on top. Brush with same olive oil thyme was soaked in. Proof and bake at 380°F/190°C. Cut into bite-size slivers. See photo on page 123.

#H 125

Wild Mushroom Brioche

Fill baked brioche with wild mushroom puree, recipe #R 158, page 68.

Cream cheese dough products

The easiest and quickest dough to make is cream cheese dough.

See recipe #HT 101 cream cheese dough and step by step directions for making croissants on page 29.

Cream cheese dough can be flavored with many spices, such as paprika, cumin, chili, and also chopped herbs. The flavors are added when the dough is prepared or to the finished dough. Fresh herbs must be squeezed very dry otherwise the dough gets too wet.

Between ¼ and ½ cup (0.06 to 0.11 l) of spice should be added to the basic recipe according to taste. Like all dough, cream cheese dough should rest refrigerated everytime something is added. The dough freezes well.

The following items can also be made with flaky yeast or dough.

Cabbage and Dill Croissants   **#H 126**

Yield: 50 pieces

cabbage and dill filling, recipe #R 133, page 56
cream cheese dough #HT 101, page 29
egg wash

Roll dough about ¼ in. (7 mm) thick, cut in triangles, fill, roll into croissants, egg wash and bake at 425°F/215°C.

*Ham and sherry croissants recipe
#H 127, this page.*

#H 127 Ham and Sherry Croissants

Yield: 50 pieces

> *ham and sherry filling #R 154, page 66*
> *cream cheese dough #HT 101, page 29*
> *egg wash*

Roll dough about ¼ in. (7 mm) dough thick, cut into triangles, fill, roll into croissants, egg wash, bake at 425°F/215°C.

Note: Make sure filling is chilled before use.

Pancetta (Italian Bacon) and Savoy Cabbage Croissants

#H 128

Yield: 50 pieces

> *pancetta filling #R 138, page 59*
> *cream cheese dough #HT 101, page 29*
> *egg wash*

Roll dough about ¼ in. (7 mm) dough thick, cut in triangles, fill, roll into croissants, egg wash and bake at 425°F/215°C.

Minted Lamb Silver Dollars

#H 129

Yield: 100

> *lamb and pignoli filling recipe #R 137, page 58*
> *flaky yeast dough recipe #HT 103, page 34*
> *egg wash*

Roll dough about ¼ in. (7 mm) thick, cut 100 circles, 1 in. (25 mm) egg wash, place 1 tsp filling on top, bake at 400°F/200°C.

Note: Filling will get solid if refrigerated. Warm slightly before placing it on dough circles.

#H 130   ## Pissaladiere

Yield: 150 pieces

¼ cup	0.06 l	fresh rosemary leaves
¼ cup	0.06 l	olive oil
		flaky yeast dough recipe #HT 103, page 34
1 cup	0.23 l	black olives, pitted and coarsely chopped, pickled in oil
1 cup	0.23 l	tomatoes, peeled, seeded, and diced
20	20	anchovy fillets
½ cup	0.11 l	Parmesan cheese, grated

Soak rosemary leaves in olive oil. Roll yeast dough about ¼ in. (7 mm) thick and cut into strips about 2½ in. (62 mm) wide. Sprinkle with oil soaked rosemary leaves. Sprinkle with olives and tomatoes. Top with anchovy fillets arranged in an attractive pattern and sprinkle with cheese. Bake at 450°F/220°C. Cut into small slices.

Note: Pissaladiere is a dish from southern France and is related to pizza. It can be made with different dough.

#H 131   ## Silver Dollars with Anchovy and Pesto

Yield: 48

		cream cheese dough recipe #HT 101, page 29
4	4	Italian plum tomatoes
¼ cup	0.06 l	black olives, chopped
8	8	anchovy fillets
¼ cup	0.06 l	prepared pesto
½ cup	0.11 l	grated cheese

Roll dough about ¼ in. (7 mm) thick and cut into 1½ in. (37 mm) circles. Slice tomatoes in half and cut each half into 6 slices. Put on dough circles, top with pesto and grated cheese. Cut each anchovy fillet into 8 pieces and put on top. Bake at 400°F/200°C until crisp.

Note: Pesto is best purchased ready to use or see pesto, recipe #R 170, page 74.

Silver Dollars with Anise Seeds and Lemon Peel   #H 132

Yield: 50 pieces

3	3	*rinds of large lemons*
		cream cheese dough recipe
		#HT 101, page 29
		or
		flaky yeast dough, (half
		amount) recipe #HT
		103, page 34
3 tbsp	3 tbsp	*anise seeds*
		egg wash

Grate lemon rind. Roll out dough about ⅜ in. (9 mm) thick, sprinkle with lemon rind, fold twice and refrigerate 1 hour. Chop anise seeds. Roll out dough about ⅜ in. (9 mm) thick and cut 50 round pieces 1½ in. (37 mm) across. Paint silver dollars with egg wash, sprinkle with anise seeds, and bake at 400°F/200°C.

Silver Dollars with Blue Cheese, Apples, and Walnuts   #H 133

Yield: 50 pieces

cream cheese dough recipe #HT 101, page 29
blue cheese, apple, and walnut filling recipe #R 131, page 55
egg wash

Roll out dough about ¼ in. (7 mm) thick and cut circles 1 in. (25 mm) across. Egg wash. Top with filling. Bake at 400°F/200°C.

Silver dollars with cheddar cheese recipe #H 134, this page.

#H 134   Silver Dollars with Cheddar Cheese

Yield: 50

		cream cheese dough recipe #HT 101, page 29
½ cup	0.11 l	*chopped herbs*
		egg wash
50	50	*cheese circles the same size as the dough circles*
		chives

Mix dough with herbs, rest overnight in refrigerator. Roll out dough about ¼ in. (7 mm) thick and cut circles 1½ in. (37 mm) across. Egg wash. Place sprig of chives in center. Top with cheese. Bake at 400°F/200°C.

Note: When cheese is melted chives will show through.

Silver Dollars with Onion Confit

Yield: 50

> *cream cheese dough recipe #HT 101, page 29*
>   *or*
> *flaky yeast dough recipe #HT 103, page 34*
> *onion confit recipe #R 177, page 78*

Roll dough ¼ in. (7 mm) thick and cut 50 circles 1½ in. (37 mm) each. Top circles with onion mixture. Bake at low heat.

Note: The onions contain sugar and could burn if not baked at low heat. If necessary the silver dollars should be covered with aluminum foil.

Silver Dollars with Poppy Seed

Yield: 50

		cream cheese dough recipe
		#HT 101, page 29
2 tbsp	*2 tbsp*	*Hungarian paprika*
6 tbsp	*6 tbsp*	*poppy seeds*
		egg wash

Roll out dough about ⅜ in. (9 mm) thick and cut 50 round pieces 1½ in. (37 mm) across. Mix egg with equal amount cold water. Blend paprika and poppy seeds. Paint silver dollars, sprinkle with seed mixture, and bake at 400°F/200°C.

#H 137   # Sun-dried Tomato Silver Dollars (Miniature Pizza)

Yield: 50

1	1	egg
2 tbsp	2 tbsp	cream
50	50	flaky yeast dough circles, 1½ in. (37 mm) wide, ¼ in. (7 mm) thick, recipe #HT 103, page 34
50 slices	50 slices	plum tomatoes
50 slices	50 slices	mozzarella cheese, cured, cut in 1½ in. (37 mm) circles
½ cup	0.11 l	sun-dried tomato pesto basil leaves

Break egg and mix with cream. Paint top of dough circles. Top with tomatoes, mozzarella cheese, and a dab of sun-dried tomato pesto. Proof and bake. Garnish with basil leaves before service.

Plate with seven sun-dried tomato silver dollars (miniature pizza) recipe #H 137, this page.

Silver Dollars with Smoked Salmon   **#H 138**

Yield: 50

4 oz	112 g	cream cheese
½ cup	0.11 l	sour cream
¼ cup	0.06 l	horseradish, grated and drained
¼ cup	0.06 l	fresh dill, chopped
50	50	flaky yeast dough circles, 1½ in. (37 cm) wide, ¼ in. (7 mm) thick, recipe #HT 103, page 34
50	50	smoked salmon slices, about 2½ x 1 in. (62 x 25 mm)

Combine all ingredients except salmon. Put about 1 tsp on each dough circle. Top with salmon, folded so it will cover circle nicely. Bake at 425°F/220°C.

Silver Dollars with Sesame Seeds   **#H 139**

Yield: 50 pieces

cream cheese dough recipe #HT 101, page 29
  or
flaky yeast dough recipe #HT 103, page 34
white sesame seeds
black sesame seeds
egg wash

Roll out dough about ¼ in. (7 mm) thick and cut 50 circles 1½ in. (37 mm) across. Paint silver dollars with egg wash, cover evenly one half with white, the other half with black seeds. Bake at 400°F/200°C.

#H 140

Smoked Trout and Spinach Croissants

Yield: 50 pieces

> *cream cheese dough recipe #HT 101, page 29*
> *smoked trout and spinach filling recipe #R 144, page 62*
> *egg wash*

Roll dough ¼ in. (7 mm) thick, cut in triangles, fill, roll into croissants, egg wash, and bake at 425°F/225°C.

#H 141

Smoked Whitefish and Chives Croissants

Yield: 50

> *smoked whitefish and chive filling recipe #R 145, page 62*
> *cream cheese dough recipe #HT 101, page 29*
> *egg wash*

Roll dough about ¼ in. (7 mm) thick, cut in triangles, fill, roll into croissants, egg wash and bake at 425°F/225°C.

#H 142

Strudel with Onion Confit

Yield: 50 pieces

> *cream cheese dough recipe #HT 101, page 29*
> *egg wash*
> *onion confit recipe #R 177, page 77*

Roll cream cheese dough ¼ in. (7 mm) thick and cut into strips 3½ in. (90 mm) wide. Brush with egg wash. Fill strip with cold onion confit, fold dough over and egg wash again. Let egg wash dry about 20 minutes and decorate top with fork. Bake until brown. Cut into bite-size pieces.

Cream puff products

Cream puffs, also called profiterole in French, are standard products in pastry shops. The basic paste is not sweet and can be filled with many different fillings, served hot or cold. Cream puff paste can also be fried, and a number of cream puff paste recipes are in the fried food section.

See basic recipe #R 107, page 44.

Alaskan Crabmeat Cream Puff Pearls #H 143

Yield: 100 pieces

32 oz	900 g	Alaskan crabmeat, frozen, flakes and pieces
1 tbsp	1 tbsp	crab seasoning
1 tbsp	1 tbsp	paprika
		cream puff paste recipe #R 107, page 44
		egg wash

Defrost crabmeat, drain. Chop in food processor. Combine dough with crabmeat and seasoning. Dress small pearls on baking paper and bake at 400°F/200°C until brown. Product can be egg washed and decorated with a fork.

Note: Mixture is hard to dress with a bag, using a small #30 scoop is helpful. Pearls can also be deep-fried.

Escargots Cream Puff Pearls #H 144

Yield: 50

50	50	cream puffs, small, baked escargot filling recipe #R 151, page 65

Take top off cream puffs and place one escargot in each. Serve at once.

#H 145

Parmesan and Swiss Cheese Pearls

Yield: 100 pieces

		cream puff paste recipe #R 107, page 44
10 oz	*280 g*	*Swiss cheese, very small dice*
1 cup	*0.23 l*	*Parmesan cheese*
1 tsp	*1 tsp*	*cayenne pepper*
1 tbsp	*1 tbsp*	*prepared mustard*

Combine dough, while still warm but not hot, with cheeses, mustard, and pepper. Dress small pearls with pastry bag on baking paper and bake at 400°F/200°C until dry and brown. Product can be egg washed and decorated with a fork.

Note: Parmesan and Swiss Cheese pearls can also be fried.

#H 146

Baked Pesto Cream Puff Pearls

Yield: 100 pieces

		cream puff paste recipe #R 107, page 44
1 cup	*0.23 l*	*prepared pesto or recipe #R 170, page 74*

Combine dough with pesto. Dress small pearls with pastry bag on baking paper and bake at 400°F/200°C until dry and brown. Product can be egg washed and decorated with a fork.

Note: Item can also be deep-fried.

Filo dough products

Filo dough, also spelled phyllo dough, and called Strudel dough in German, is a very thin, almost transparent dough. It can be made on premise but is best purchased ready to use. Recipe #HT 102 for filo dough and directions for use of purchased dough can be found on page 32.

Filo dough can be shaped into bundles, strudels, triangles, turnovers, or nests.

Blue Cheese, Apples, and Walnuts Bundles   **#H 147**

Yield: 80 pieces

8 oz	*225 g*	*butter*
10 sheets	*10 sheets*	*filo dough, recipe #HT 102, page 32*
		blue cheese, apples, and walnut filling recipe #R 130, page 55

Melt butter. Make bundles or triangles according to instructions on page 32.

Brie Cheese and Sun-dried Tomato Pesto Bundles   **#H 148**

Yield: 80 pieces

		Brie cheese and sun-dried tomato pesto recipe #R 132, page 56
10 sheets	*10 sheets*	*filo dough*
½ cup	*0.12 l*	*olive oil*

Fill filo bundles with cheese filling.

#H 149

Cabbage and Dill Bundles (vegetarian)

Yield: 80 pieces

8 oz	*225 g*	*butter*
10	*10*	*filo dough sheets, recipe*
		#HT 102, page 32
		cabbage and dill filling
		recipe #R 133, page 56

Melt butter. Make bundles or triangles according to instructions on page 32.

#H 150

Cauliflower Bundles (vegetarian)

Yield: 80 pieces

8 oz	*225 g*	*butter*
10	*10*	*filo dough sheets, recipe*
		#HT 102, page 32
		cauliflower filling recipe
		#R 134, page 57

Melt butter. Make bundles or triangles according to instructions on page 32.

Escargots in Filo Cups

#H 151

Yield: 48

24	24	*filo dough sheets*
16 oz	450 g	*butter*
¼ tsp	¼ tsp	*garlic*
2 tbsp	2 tbsp	*shallots*
¼ cup	0.06 l	*olive oil*
48	48	*large escargots (snails)*
2 tbsp	2tbsp	*Pernod*
1 cup	0.23 l	*spinach, pureed*
1 cup	0.23 l	*watercress, pureed*
		salt and pepper to taste

Make filo cups as explained in recipe #HT 102, page 32 and in recipe #H 156, page 143. Saute garlic and shallots in oil. Drain snails and marinate with oil mixture and Pernod. Warm snails, drain marinade and mix marinade with spinach and watercress puree. Warm vegetable puree and season with pepper and salt. Use pastry bag and fill cups with vegetable puree, top with warm snail. The item should be assembled as needed and will get soggy when standing.

Note: If a large amount of filo cups must be filled ahead of time a small circle of thin white bread can be place at the bottom of each cup. This will soak up any juices. The vegetable puree should more highly seasoned to compensate for the bland flavor of the bread.

Goat Cheese and Broccoli Rabe Triangles

#H 152

Yield: 80 pieces

1 tbsp	1 tbsp	*shallots*
1 tsp	1 tsp	*garlic, chopped*
1 tbsp	1 tbsp	*oil*
1 cup	0.23 l	*broccoli rabe, washed and chopped*
		salt and pepper to taste
16 oz	450 g	*goat cheese*
8 oz	225 g	*butter*
10	10	*filo dough sheets*

Combine shallots, garlic, and oil in heavy saucepan with lid. Sweat shallots until transparent. Add broccoli, season to taste and cover. Steam 5 minutes or until the vegetable is cooked. Drain if wet. Cool filling. Add goat cheese, mix thoroughly. Melt butter. Make bundles or triangles.

#H 153

Ham and Sherry Wine Bundles

Yield: 80 pieces

8 oz	225 g	butter
10	10	filo dough sheets
		double ham and sherry wine filling recipe #R 154, page 66

Melt butter. Make bundles or triangles according to instructions on page 32. Make sure filling is chilled.

#H 154

Pancetta and Savoy Cabbage Bundles

Yield: 80 pieces

8 oz	225 g	butter
10	10	filo dough sheets
		double pancetta and savoy cabbage filling recipe #R 138, page 59

Melt butter. Make bundles or triangles according to instructions on page 32.

#H 155

Oyster Rockefeller Strudel

Yield: 80 portions

10	10	filo dough sheets
8 oz	225 g	butter, melted
		Oyster Rockefeller filling recipe #R 141, page 60
		egg wash

Put double layer of filo dough on damp (not wet) towel. Brush with butter. Place filling on about two-thirds of dough, brush remaining dough with butter. Lift towel and roll into a strudel (roll), the unfilled portion of dough should be the outer layers. Brush with butter and bake. Let rest before cutting into 1 in. (25 mm) pieces for service.

Sea Scallops in Filo Cups

Yield: 48 servings

4	4	filo dough sheets
10 oz	280 g	butter
2 cups	0.46 l	cucumbers, peeled, seeded, and diced small
½ cup	0.11 l	red pepper, diced small
2 tbsp	2 tbsp	prepared mustard
1 tsp	1 tsp	sugar
		salt and pepper to taste
48	48	sea scallops, bite-size
		oil

Cut each filo sheet into 3 in. (75 mm) squares. Melt butter, butter small muffin tins, and put four sheets each into each tin. Butter lightly on the inside and trim off excessive dough. Fill each cup with dried beans or peas and blind bake. Remove legumes while cups are still hot. Make sure cucumbers and peppers are cut into small dice. Just before service season with mustard, sugar, pepper, and salt. Grill or broil scallops, they should be

On lower side of plate are sea scallops in filo cups recipe #H 156, on upper side are escargots in filo cups recipe #H 151, page 141.

hot but not fully cooked. Fill cups with cucumber mixture and place scallop on top. The item should be assembled as needed and will get soggy when standing.

Note: For directions about how to work with filo dough refer to page 32. If a large amount of filo cups must be filled ahead of time a small circle of thin white bread can be placed at the bottom of each cup. This will soak up any juices. The cucumber mixture should be seasoned more highly to compensate for the bland flavor of the bread.

#H 157

Smoked Trout and Spinach Bundles

Yield: 80 pieces

8 oz	225 g	*butter*
10	10	*filo dough sheets*
		double smoked trout and
		spinach filling recipe #R
		144, page 62

Melt butter. Make bundles or triangles according to instructions on page 32.

Smoked trout and spinach bundles recipe #H 157, this page, and blue cheese, apples, and walnuts bundles recipe #H 147, page 139.

Smoked whitefish and chive purses, recipe #H 158, this page.

145

HOT HORS D'OEUVRES

Smoked Whitefish and Chive Purses

#H 158

Yield: 80 pieces

8 oz	225 g	*butter*
10	10	*filo dough sheets*
		double smoked whitefish and chive filling recipe #R 145, page 62

Melt butter. Make bundles or triangles according to instructions on page 32.

Croustades

The correct definition of a croustade is a crisp, baked or fried edible container. It can be made of filo dough, polenta, bread, and other ingredients.

The term is also commonly used for thin, hot, open-faced sandwiches on crisp french bread, also called baguette or flute.

#H 159

Croustade (Cups) with Papaya and Red Pepper Coulis (vegetarian)

Yield: 50

2 cups	0.46 l	papaya, cut in small dice
1 tsp	1 tsp	amchoor powder
2 cups	0.46 l	red pepper coulis recipe #R 159, page 69
50	50	croustade shells made with filo dough recipe #HT 102, page 143

Combine papaya with amchoor powder and keep at room temperature. Warm red pepper coulis. Fill hot croustades first with a layer papaya and top with red pepper coulis. Serve at once.

#H 160

Baguette Croustades of Chevre Cheese

Yield: 50

50 each	50 each	chevre cheese, slices
2	2	egg whites
50 each	50 each	baguette slices, ⅛ in. (4 mm)
		oil
½ cup	0.11 l	prepared mustard
1 cup	0.23 l	poppy seeds

Chill cheese so it can be handled. Mix egg whites with equal amount of water. Brush bread with oil, arrange on baking sheet, and bake until brown. Put dab of mustard on each slice. Dip cheese slices in egg whites and dredge in poppy seeds. Place on toasted bread slices. Bake as needed.

Baguette Croustade with Ham Mousse and Orange Marmalade

Yield: 50 pieces

50	50	baguette slices, *about 1½ in. (37 mm) across and ⅛ in. (4 mm) thick*
½ cup	0.11 l	olive oil
1 cup	0.23 l	orange marmalade
3 cups	0.70 l	ham and sherry filling recipe #R 154, page 66

Brush baguette slices on both sides with oil, place on baking sheet, and toast until brown. Warm orange marmalade and spread each slice with brush. Spread ham mousse with spatula on each slice and bake until hot.

The platter displays 5 croustades made on baguette bread. They are from right to left: baguette croustade with broiled prunes with blue cheese recipe #H 224, page 184; baguette croustade with smoked salmon and coriander spinach, recipe #H 164, page 149; baguette croustade with herb poultry mousse and black sesame seeds, #H 163, page 148; ham mousse with orange marmelade, #H 161, page 147; and black and white mushroom mousse, #H 162, page 148.

#H 162 | ## Baguette Croustade with Black and White Mushroom Mousse (vegetarian)

Yield: 50

50	50	baguette slices, about 1½ in. (37 mm) across and ⅛ in. (4 mm) thick
½ cup	0.11 l	olive oil
1½ cup	0.34 l	white mushroom mousse recipe #R 157, page 68
1½ cup	0.34 l	black (wild) mushroom mousse recipe #R 158 page 68

Brush baguette slices on both sides with oil, place on baking sheet and toast until brown. Spread white and black mushroom mousse with spatula on each slice and bake until hot.

#H 163 | ## Baguette Croustade with Herb Poultry Mousse and Black Sesame Seeds

Yield: 50

50	50	baguette slices, about 1½ in. (37 mm) across and ⅛ in. (4 mm) thick
½ cup	0.11 l	olive oil
3 cups	0.70 l	poultry mousse recipe #R 140, page 60
½ cup	0.11 l	herbs of choice, chopped, primarily parsley
½ cup	0.12 l	black sesame seeds

Brush baguette slices on both sides with oil, place on baking sheet, and toast until brown. Mix poultry mousse with chopped herbs. Spread poultry mousse with spatula on each slice, dip upside down in sesame seeds, and bake at 375°F/190°C about 10 minutes. See picture on page 147.

Baguette Croustade with Smoked Salmon and Coriander Spinach

Yield: 50 pieces

50	50	baguette slices, about 1½ in. (37 mm) across and ⅛ in. (4 mm) thick
½ cup	0.11 l	olive oil
2 tbsp	2 tbsp	coriander
3 cups	0.70 l	spinach filling recipe #R 146, page 63
18	18	smoked salmon, slices

Brush baguette slices on both sides with oil, place on baking sheet, and toast until brown. Crush coriander seeds and dry toast in frying pan until lightly toasted. Mix with spinach filling. Spread spinach filling with spatula on each slice. Cut salmon slices in three pieces each, place one piece on each croustade. Bake in oven until heated (see photo on page 147).

Baguette Croustade of Tomatoes and Oregano

Yield: 50 pieces

¾ cup	0.17 l	sun-dried tomatoes
¼ cup	0.06 l	shallots, chopped
½ cup	0.11 l	olive oil
2 tbsp	2 tbsp	tomato paste
1 tsp	1 tsp	fresh oregano, chopped
1 cup	0.23 l	tomatoes, peeled, seeded, and diced
		salt and pepper
50	50	baguette slices, about 1½ in. (37 mm) across

Cover sun-dried tomatoes with water and soak overnight. Bring to boil and cook 30 minutes until soft. Drain. Chop to coarse consistency in food processor. Saute shallots in 3 tbsp oil until light brown, add tomato paste, oregano, and sun-dried tomatoes. Stir over heat until well blended, season. Remove from heat, add diced tomatoes, keep warm. Brush baguette slices on both sides with oil, place on baking sheet and toast until brown. Put 1 tsp mixture on each slice as needed.

Note: Canned peeled tomatoes, well squeezed, can be substituted for the fresh peeled tomatoes.

#H 166

Baguette Croustade with Tomatoes and Swiss Cheese

Yield: 50

¾ cup	0.17 l	sun-dried tomatoes
¼ cup	0.06 l	shallots, chopped
½ cup	0.11 l	olive oil
2 tbsp	2 tbsp	tomato paste
1 tbsp	1 tbsp	fresh basil, chopped
1 cup	0.23 l	Swiss cheese, diced
½ cup	0.11 l	cheese, grated
		salt and pepper
50	50	baguette slices, about 1½ in. (37 mm) across

Cover sun-dried tomatoes with water and soak overnight. Bring to boil and cook 30 minutes until soft. Drain. Chop to coarse consistency in food processor. Saute shallots in 3 tbsp oil until light brown, add tomato paste, basil, and sun-dried tomatoes. Stir over heat until well blended, season. Cool. Add cheeses. Brush baguette slices on both sides with oil, place on baking sheet, and toast until brown. Put 1 tsp mixture on each slice as needed and bake until hot. Garnish with basil leaves.

#H 167

Baguette Croustade with Zucchini and Tomatoes

Yield: 50

¾ cup	0.17 l	sun-dried tomatoes
¼ cup	0.06 l	shallots, chopped
½ cup	0.11 l	olive oil
2 tbsp	2 tbsp	tomato paste
1 tbsp	1 tbsp	fresh basil, chopped
		salt and pepper
1½ cups	0.34 l	zucchini, small diced
½ cup	0.11 l	cheese, grated
50	50	baguette slices, 1½ in. (37 mm) across

Cover sun-dried tomatoes with water and soak overnight. Bring to boil and cook 30 minutes until soft. Drain. Chop to coarse consistency in food processor. Saute shallots in 3 tbsp oil until light brown, add tomato paste, basil, and sun-dried tomatoes. Stir over heat until well blended, season. Cool. Add zucchini. Brush baguette slices on both sides with oil, place on baking sheet and toast until brown. Put 1 tsp mixture on each slice as needed, sprinkle with grated cheese and bake until hot. Garnish with basil leaves.

Bread Croustade with Tapenade #H 168

Yield: 50

½ cup	0.12 l	olive oil
50	50	sandwich bread, sliced thin
2 cups	0.46 l	tapenade recipe #R 163, page 71
2	2	eggs

Brush small muffin molds with oil. Place bread slices in molds and trim off rim. Mix tapenade with 2 eggs. Fill molds with tapenade and bake at 400°F/200°C until brown.

Muffins

Small muffins with different flavors are attractive hors d'oeuvres when passed butler style. There are many different muffin molds on the market.

For weddings, small heart shaped muffins passed during the reception can be delightful. These can be brushed with egg white diluted with water after baking, while still hot and covered with vark (edible gold or silver foil available in Indian stores).

Blue Corn Muffins with Jalapeño Peppers #H 169

Yield: 80 pieces

recipe #R 117 blue corn muffins, page 49
Jalapeño peppers according to taste

Add diced peppers to batter.

Note: Jalapeño peppers can be very hot!

Corn Muffins with Sunflower Seeds #H 170

Yield: 80 pieces

		recipe #R 117 blue corn muffins, page 49
1½ cups	0.34 l	sunflower seeds

Add sunflower seeds to batter.

#H 171

Corn Muffins with Chili and Dried Cranberries

Yield: 80 pieces

		corn muffin recipe #R 116, page 48
2 cups	*0.46 l*	*dried cranberries*
1 tsp	*1 tsp*	*chili powder*

Mix dried cranberries with chili powder and blend into muffin mixture. Fill small muffin molds and bake.

#H 172

Corn Muffin with Cheese Curd

Yield: 80

corn muffin recipe #R 116, page 48
cheese curd recipe #R 148, page 63

Cut off top of baked muffins, add cheese curd with pastry bag, close top, and serve warm.

#H 173

Corn Muffins with Herbs and Spices

Yield: 80 pieces

corn muffin recipe #R 116, page 48
spices or herbs

The batter can be flavored with a wide range of spices or herbs, such as chili powder, chopped cilantro, hot pepper flakes, fresh or dried herbs.

Corn Muffins with Red Caviar and Sour Cream

#H 174

Yield: 80 pieces

		corn muffin recipe #R 116, page 48
16 oz	0.46 l	sour cream
8–10 oz	225–280 g	red caviar (or any other caviar)
		dill

Bake muffins. Hollow out muffins and fill with sour cream and caviar just before service. Garnish with dill.

Note: If muffins are too hot sour cream will melt.

Corn muffins with red caviar and sour cream recipe #H 174, this page.

#H 175   Muffins with Bacon and Cheese

Yield: 50 pieces

32 oz	900 g	bacon
2 tbsp	2 tbsp	onions, chopped
2 tbsp	2 tbsp	chives, chopped
16 oz	450 g	cake flour
1 tbsp	1 tbsp	baking powder
1 cup	0.23 l	Parmesan cheese, grated
6 oz	170 g	butter or margarine, melted
2	2	eggs
1 cup	0.23 l	buttermilk

Cook bacon until crisp, drain and cool. When cool, chop and crumble. Saute onions in 2 tbsp bacon fat, add to bacon. Add chives. Combine dry ingredients. Mix wet ingredients. Combine both to make batter. Do not whip. Add bacon mixture. Fill in tiny muffin tins and bake.

Three muffin varieties. Starting on the right: muffins with bacon and cheese recipe #H 175, this page; corn muffins with sunflower seeds #H 170, page 151; muffins with spices #H 173, page 152.

Muffins with poppy seeds recipe #R 118, on bread and butter plate. Muffins are bite size.

Muffins with Poppy Seeds

#H 176

Yield: 80 pieces

muffin recipe #R 118, page 49

Note: Poppy seeds can be substituted with sunflower or pumpkin seeds, and crushed nuts.

#H 177   ## Oatmeal Sesame Silver Dollars

Yield: 100

5 cups	1.15 l	rolled oats
1 cup	0.23 l	flour
½ cup	0.11 l	oil
2 tbsp	2 tbsp	sesame oil
2 cups	0.46 l	sesame seeds
2 cups	0.46 l	water

Combine ingredients. Place small amounts of mixture on oiled cookie sheet, flatten, and bake at 375°F/190°C until brown and crisp.

#H 178   ## Polenta Bruschetta

Yield: 50 pieces

1 tbsp	1 tbsp	olive oil
1 tsp	1 tsp	garlic, chopped
1½ cups	0.34 l	tomatoes, peeled and seeded
1 tbsp	1 tbsp	tomato paste
2 tbsp	2 tbsp	basil leaves, chopped
1 tsp	1 tsp	sugar
1 tsp	1 tsp	butcher ground pepper
1½ cups	0.34 l	mozzarella cheese, grated polenta recipe #R 121, page 51

Saute garlic in oil. Chop tomatoes and all other ingredients except cheese and polenta. Cook over high heat, stirring frequently until mixture is rather dry. Cool. Cut polenta into bite-size pieces, top with tomato mixture, sprinkle with cheese, and bake until brown.

Semolina Tidbits with Pesto

Yield: 100

32 oz (4 cups)	0.93 l	milk
2 oz	60 g	butter
1½ cups	0.34 l	semolina (coarse cream of wheat)
½ tsp	½ tsp	salt
¼ tsp	¼ tsp	nutmeg
1 cup	0.23 l	cheese, grated
1 cup	0.23 l	pesto, purchased or recipe #R 170, page 74
4	4	eggs yolks
		oil

Bring milk and butter to boil, add salt and nutmeg. Pour semolina in steady stream into milk, stir well, bring to boil again, cover and cook over very low heat, about 10 minutes. Take off heat, add pesto, cheese, and eggs, stir well. Spread mixture on oiled sheet pan about ½ in. (12 mm) high, cover will foil and cool. When cold, cut into attractive shapes and bake on oiled sheet pans until crisp and brown.

Popovers

Popover with Finnan Haddie recipe #H 180, this page.

#H 180

Popover with Finnan Haddie

Yield: 50 pieces

> *basic popover recipe #R 122 page 51*
> *Finnan Haddie in cream sauce recipe #R 153, page 66*
> *capers*

Make popovers. Cut out top, push in center, and fill cavity of popovers as needed. Garnish with capers.

#H 181

Popover with Onion Confit

Yield: 50 pieces

> *basic popover recipe #R 122, page 51*
> *onion confit recipe #R 177, page 78*

Fill popovers with onion confit.

Popover with salmon caviar recipe #H 182, this page.

Popover with Salmon Caviar   **#H 182**

Yield: 50 pieces

		basic popover recipe #R 122, page 51
16 oz	0.46 l	sour cream
8 oz	280 g	salmon caviar
		dill sprigs

Make popovers according to recipe. Make sure they are well dried out. Keep at room temperature. At moment of service, fill popovers with sour cream and caviar, garnish with dill sprig.

Note: If popovers are hot, the sour cream will melt and the items will be messy. The concept works when popovers are very dry, at room temperature, and filled as needed.

#H 183

Popover with Sap Sago Cheese

Yield: 50

| | | *basic popover recipe #R 122, page 51* |
| 8 oz | 280 g | *Sap Sago cheese, grated* |

Combine grated cheese with batter and process according to directions on page 51.

#H 184

Popover with Shrimp and Dill Filling

Yield: 50

basic popover recipe #R 122, page 51
shrimp and dill filling recipe #R 162, page 70

At moment of service, fill popovers with hot shrimp and dill filling.

Popover with shrimp and dill filling recipe #R 162, page 70.

Popover with salmon, basil, and mustard filling recipe #H 185, this page.

Popover with Salmon, Basil, and Mustard Filling #H 185

Yield: 50

basic popover recipe #R 122, page 51
salmon, basil, and mustard filling recipe #R 161, page 70

At moment of service, fill popovers with hot salmon, basil, and mustard filling.

Popover with Whitefish, Apple, and Caper Filling #H 186

Yield: 50

basic popover recipe #R 122, page 51
whitefish, apple, and caper filling recipe #R 165, page 72

At moment of service, fill popovers with whitefish, apple, and caper filling.

Tartlets

Tartlets should be made with a short dough which should not get soggy when filled, but is crumbly enough to be eaten with gusto. Tartlets can be purchased ready baked in many sizes and made with different dough varieties.

Recipe #HT 104 and directions for working with shell (tartlet) dough are on page 35.

#H 187   Tartlets with Three Cheeses

Yield: 100 pieces

		cream puff paste recipe #R 107, page 44
1 cup	0.23 l	Swiss cheese, very small dice
1 cup	0.23 l	Parmesan cheese, grated
1 cup	0.23 l	blue cheese, crumbled
100	100	tartlets, not baked, made with shell dough recipe #HT 104, page 35

Combine cream puff paste with cheese. Paste should be room temperature; if too hot cheese will melt and filling the tartlet will be difficult. Fill tartlet with cream puff paste and bake at 400°F/200°C.

#H 188   Tartlets with Clams

Yield: 100 pieces

1½ cups	0.11 l	clam juice
24 oz	0.70 l	canned clams, drained and chopped
1 cup	0.23 l	dehydrated potato powder
1 tbsp	1 tbsp	oil
2	2	egg yolks
½ cup	0.11 l	chives
		salt and pepper to taste
100	100	tartlets, not baked recipe #HT 104, page 35

Heat clam juice, add all ingredients, mix well. Fill unbaked shells with mixture, bake at 400°F/200°C.

Tartlets with Crabmeat   #H 189

Yield: 50

24 oz	675 g	Maryland crabmeat
1½ cup	0.11 l	mayonnaise
3 tbsp	3 tbsp	prepared mustard
3 tbsp	3 tbsp	chives, diced
50	50	tartlets, baked, recipe #HT 104, page 35

Pick bones and shells from crabmeat, drain. Combine with remaining ingredients and fill tartlet shells. Heat in oven as needed.

Note: Keep mixture chilled until use. Maryland crabmeat is very expensive; less expensive crabmeat can be substituted.

Tartlets with Curried Beef and Chutney   #H 190

Yield: 50 pieces

		curried beef and chutney filling, recipe #R 149, page 64
50	50	tartlets, baked, recipe #HT 104, page 35

Fill tartlets with curried beef mixture.

Tartlets Filled with Escargots   #H 191

Yield: 48

		escargots filling recipe #R 150, page 64
		or
		escargots filling recipe #R 151, page 65
48	48	tartlets, baked, recipe #HT 104, page 35

Fill tartlets with escargots when needed and serve hot.

#H 192

Tartlets with Feta Cheese and Apples

Yield: 50 pieces

2	2	*lemons*
16 oz	450 g	*feta cheese, drained*
1½ cups	0.34 l	*apples, small dice*
50	50	*tartlets, baked, recipe* *#HT 104, page 35*

Grate lemon peel and squeeze juice. Crumble or chop feta cheese and combine with lemon peel, lemon juice, and apples. Fill tartlets and bake at low heat until cheese melts.

#H 193

Tartlets with Miso

Yield: 50 pieces

		miso filling recipe #R 155, *page 67*
50	50	*tartlets, baked, recipe* *#HT 104, page 35*

Fill tartlets with miso.

Note: Miso is very salty.

An assortment of tartlets is presented on a platter to be served butler style. Bottom row: poultry mousse #H 194, page 165; brie cheese and sundried tomatoes, #R 132, page 56; turkey mole filling #R 164, page 71; blue cheese, apple and walnut, #R 131, page 55; curried beef and chutney filling, #H 190, page 163. The pink tartlets are filled with miso, #R 155, page 67.

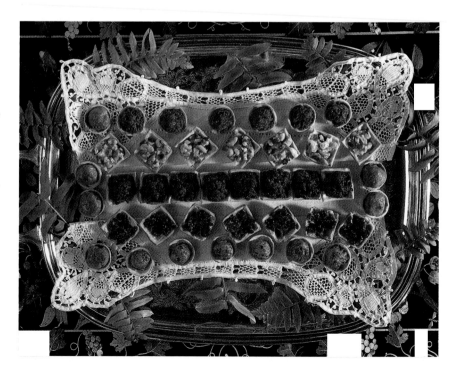

Tartlets with Poultry Mousse

Yield: 50 pieces

50	50	tartlets, not baked, recipe #HT 104, page 35 poultry mousse recipe #R 140, page 60

Fill tartlets generously with poultry mousse and bake.

Note: Use pastry bag to fill tartlets. If tartlets are prebaked they will get less soggy.

Tartlets with Oriental Shrimp Mousse

Yield: 150 pieces

150	150	tartlets, not baked, recipe #HT 104, page 35 seafood Oriental filling recipe #R 142, page 61

Fill tartlets with seafood filling and bake at 400°F/200°C.

Tartlets with Shrimp and Dill

Yield: 50

50	50	tartlets, baked, recipe #HT 104, page 35 shrimp and dill filling recipe #R 162, page 70

Fill tartlets with shrimp filling and heat until warm. Do not fill ahead of time. Keep filling refrigerated.

#H 197   ## Tartlets with Swiss Cheese and Dried Cherries

Yield: 50 pieces

50	50	tartlets, baked, recipe #HT 104, page 35
1½ cups	0.34 l	dried sour cherries
2 tsp	2 tsp	fresh ginger, chopped
1½ cups	0.34 l	Swiss cheese, very small dice

Chop dried cherries and combine with ginger and cheese. Fill tartlets and heat until cheese is melted.

Note: Tartlets can be filled ahead of time and heated at the last moment. Make sure to use dried sour cherries and *not candied* cherries, which are sweet. This item can be served butler style.

#H 198   ## Tartlets with Smoked Duckling

Yield: 50 pieces

16 oz	450 g	duck skin, raw (see note)
16 oz	450 g	boneless smoked duck
½ cup	0.11 l	almonds, chopped
1 cup	0.23 l	prepared mango chutney
¼ cup	0.06 l	horseradish, grated
50	50	tartlets, baked, recipe #HT 104, page 35

Oven-roast duck skin until crisp. Skin will burn easily and caution is advised. Cool and crumble into fine pieces. Dice smoked duck into small dice. Toast almonds. Puree chutney in food processor, add horseradish. Combine all ingredients. Fill tartlets with mixture as needed and warm in oven.

Note: Many restaurants buy duckling breast with skin on and serve it skinless. The breast can be used for this item. If skins are not available the back skin from roast duckling portions can be saved and used. Chicken skin is also useful. The crisp skin gives the dish the necessary texture.

Miscellaneous items

Artichoke Bottoms with Poultry Mousse   #H 199

Yield: 48 pieces

12	12	artichokes, small, with stems
2	2	lemons
		poultry mousse recipe #R 140, page 60
¼ cup	0.06 l	olive oil
½ cup	0.11 l	bread crumbs

Cut artichokes in quarters, trim outer leaves and remove center hay. Since artichokes are small, most outer leaves can be eaten. Boil in lemon water until soft, but not mushy. Cool. Remove, drain, and dry. Use pastry bag to fill inside with poultry mousse. Sprinkle with oil and bread crumbs, place on baking sheet and bake as needed for about 15 minutes.

Note: Poultry mousse can be flavored with different spices for variety. Canned or frozen artichoke hearts can be used.

Baked Filled Baby Vegetables   #H 200

vegetables of choice
fish mousse, poultry mousse, miso, or other filling of choice
oil

Cut top or bottom of vegetable and keep as lid. Scoop out vegetable. Coarsely chop vegetables that have been scooped out and steam for 5 minutes. Chill. Mix vegetables with filling, adjust seasoning. Fill cavity generously (use pastry bag), place lid on top. Put vegetables in shallow baking pan, brush with oil, cover with foil and slow bake until filling is cooked. Pictures shows: miso, shrimp mouse, poultry mousse, and fish mousse.

Many baby vegetables can be filled. The easiest to handle are pattypan squash and tiny turnips.

Baby vegetables, filled recipe #H 200, page 167. The picture shows miniature squash filled with fish mousse recipe #R 136, page 58; and with miso filling recipe #R 155, page 67. They are shown with and without lids.

Small squash filled with shrimp spread recipe #R 143, page 61. The vegetable can be baked or steamed.

Baked Reuben Sandwich #H 201

Yield: 50 pieces

50	50	*thin white bread slices*
		mustard
100	100	*Swiss cheese, slices, about 3 x 3 in. (75 x 75 mm)*
1 cup	0.23 l	*sauerkraut, drained and chopped*
50	50	*slices corned beef, cooked, sliced thin, about 3 x 3 in. (75 x 75 mm)*
½ cup	0.11 l	*oil*

Lay 25 slices bread on table, brush with mustard. Put 1 slice cheese on each bread, top with sauerkraut, corned beef, and finish with cheese. Spread mustard on second bread slice and put on top. Cover with plastic wrap and refrigerate. Trim crust. Griddle fry or brush lightly with oil and bake. Cut in half or into triangles.

Bacalao (Salted Codfish) Cakes Made with Bread #H 202

Yield: 100

32 oz	900 g	*salted codfish (bacalao)*
32 oz	0.92 l	*milk*
32 oz	900 g	*loaf of stale white bread or white rolls*
¼ tsp	¼ tsp	*white pepper, ground*
¼ tsp	¼ tsp	*nutmeg, ground*
4	4	*eggs*
½ cup	0.11 l	*chives*
		fresh bread crumbs
		oil

Soak fish overnight in cold water. Change water once. Cut fish in ¼ in. (7 mm) dice, remove any bones. Cover fish with milk, bring to boil and simmer 20 minutes. Dice or break bread in small chunks, add to fish, add spices. Stir over fire until smooth mixture results. If bread is very dry, some milk might have to be added. Add eggs and chives, stir over heat until well mixed. Cool, shape into little balls, sprinkle with bread crumbs, and bake on oiled sheet pan.

#H 203

Bacalao (Salted Codfish) Cakes Made with Potatoes

Yield: 100 pieces

24 oz	675 g	bacalao (salted cod) fillet
5 large (40 oz)	1.10 kg	Russet potatoes
3 cups	0.70 l	milk
2	2	eggs
¼ tsp	¼ tsp	white pepper, ground
3 tbsp	3 tbsp	parsley, chopped
		flour
		oil

Soak fish in water overnight. Change water if it is still very salty. Cut fish in cubes and check for bones. Peel potatoes, dice. Combine fish and potatoes, cover with milk and cook until potatoes are done. Stir occasionally, most milk should have evaporated. Stir to break up pieces, add eggs, pepper, and parsley. If mixture is not firm enough to be shaped, add instant potato powder as needed. Place on floured pastry board and shape into dollar-size cakes. Place cakes on oiled baking sheet, sprinkle with flour, and bake as needed.

#H 204

Codfish Cakes

Yield: 80 pieces

32 oz	900 g	fresh or frozen cod fish fillets
		salt
½ cup	0.11 l	chives
1 cup	0.23 l	mayonnaise
½ cup	0.11 l	prepared mustard
1 tsp	1 tsp	dry mustard
4 cups	0.93 l	fresh bread crumbs
2	2	eggs
		oil

Cut fish in cubes, cover with water, add salt to taste, bring to boil and simmer 5 minutes. Let cool, drain, discard liquid. Flake fish and check for bones. Add remaining ingredients, blend. The amount of bread crumbs depends on wetness of fish. Mixture should be heavy. Oil baking sheet, shape cakes with scoop # 24, sprinkle with bread crumbs and oil, bake at 500°F/275°C oven until brown.

Note: Product is difficult to eat as finger food and is best served with oyster forks.

Codfish Cakes with Potatoes

Yield: 100 pieces

32 oz	900 g	fresh or frozen cod fish fillets, skin removed
5 large	1.10 kg	Russet potatoes, peeled
1	1	bay leaf
1 cup	0.23 l	chives
1 tbsp	1 tbsp	white pepper, ground
½ tsp	½ tsp	nutmeg, ground
		salt to taste
3	3	eggs
		fresh bread crumbs
		oil

Dice potatoes, cover with water. Wash fish and cut in ½ in. (12 mm) dice. Remove any residual bones. Add fish to potatoes, add bay leaf, bring to boil. Do not add more water than necessary, the fish/potato mixture should just about be covered. Simmer until fish and potatoes are done, about 20 minutes. Drain, remove bay leaf. Add all other ingredients and mash coarsely. Form balls with ice cream scoop # 24, roll in bread crumbs, flatten lightly. Place on oiled baking sheet and bake until brown.

Crab Cakes

Yield: 80 pieces

32 oz	900 g	crabmeat
½ cup	0.11 l	chives
1 cup	0.23 l	mayonnaise
4 tbsp	4 tbsp	prepared mustard
1 tsp	1 tsp	dry mustard
		salt
4 cups	0.93 l	fresh bread crumbs
2	2	eggs
		oil

Check crabmeat for bones. Add remaining ingredients, blend. The amount of bread crumbs depends on wetness of fish. Mixture should be heavy. Oil baking sheet, shape cakes with scoop # 24. Sprinkle with bread crumbs and oil, bake at 500°F/275°C oven until brown.

Note: Product is difficult to eat as finger food and is best served on buffets.

#H 207 — Dried Apricots with Poultry Mousse

Yield: 50 pieces

50	*50*	*apricot halves, large*
4 tbsp	*4 tbsp*	*amchoor powder*
		poultry mousse recipe #R 140, page 60
1 tbsp	*1tbsp*	*brandy*

Soak apricots in cold water with amchoor powder added until soft, or about 2 hours. Drain and pat dry. Mix chicken mousse with brandy. Fill each apricot half with chicken mousse. Place on oiled baking sheet and bake at 400°F/200°C.

Dried apricots with poultry mousse recipe #H 207, this page.

Dates and Pastrami

Yield: 50 pieces

50	50	*dates, large, pitted*
50	50	*pastrami, cooked, sliced very thin*
½ cup	0.11 l	*lemon juice*
¼ cup	0.06 l	*mint, chopped*

Wrap dates in pastrami slices, secure with toothpicks. Place tightly in baking pan, sprinkle with lemon juice. Cover with foil and bake until heated through. Sprinkle with mint before service.

Prunes with Ricotta Cheese and Prosciutto

Yield: 50 pieces

50	50	*dried prunes, jumbo size pitted*
4 oz	112 g	*cream cheese*
10 oz	280 g	*ricotta cheese*
2	2	*egg whites*
50	50	*prosciutto ham, thin sliced oil*

Blend cream cheese and ricotta cheese with 1 egg white. Season to taste. Stuff prunes with pastry bag, close all around, chill. Roll each plum with one slice ham. Moisten ham ends with egg white to seal. Fasten with toothpick. Place seam side down on baking pan. Brush with oil and broil until hot. Remove toothpick before serving.

Salmon with Fennel Crust recipe #H 210, this page.

#H 210

Salmon with Fennel Crust

Yield: 50 pieces

50	50	fresh salmon cubes, about 1 x 1½ in. (25 x 37 mm) thick, skin removed
1 tbsp	1 tbsp	salt
1 tbsp	1 tbsp	Pernod
16 oz	450 g	fennel bulbs (about 3), without greens
2 cups	0.46 l	fresh bread crumbs
2	2	egg whites
½ cup	0.11 l	red pepper, chopped and seeded
½ cup	0.11 l	oil

Salt salmon cubes, add Pernod and refrigerate. Coarsely chop and wash fennel, steam or braise without adding any water until soft. Puree in food processor. Return puree to heat, cook and stir until rather dry. Remove from heat, season, add egg whites and bread crumbs until thick paste forms. Boil red peppers, chill and drain. Add red peppers to mixture. Place ½ tsp fennel puree on each salmon cube, sprinkle with oil and bread crumbs. Brown in very hot oven as needed.

Note: Salmon pieces should be undercooked and stay firm. Product is difficult to pick up with fingers or toothpicks, it is best served with an oyster fork.

Salmon with Horseradish Crust

#H 211

Yield: 50

50	50	fresh salmon, cubes, about 1 x 1½ in. (25 x 37 mm) thick, skin removed
1 tbsp	1 tbsp	salt
3 cups	0.70 l	fresh bread crumbs
2 cups	0.46 l	light cream
		pinch nutmeg
		salt as needed
2	2	whole eggs
1 cup	0.23 l	processed horseradish, grated and drained
½ cup	0.11 l	oil

Salmon with horseradish crust recipe #H 211, this page.

Salt salmon cubes and refrigerate. Combine cream with nutmeg and sufficient bread crumbs to make paste. Heat and stir until mixture is thick, add bread crumbs as needed. Mixture should be of dough-like consistency. Remove from heat, add eggs and horseradish, mix well and cool. Place 1 tsp horseradish mixture on each salmon cube, sprinkle with oil and bread crumbs. Brown in very hot oven as needed.

Note: Salmon pieces should be undercooked and stay firm. Product is difficult to pick up with fingers or toothpicks, it is best served with a plate.

#H 212

Scallops with Mustard Seeds

Yield: 50 pieces

25	25	*large scallops*
½ tbsp	½ tbsp	*salt*
50	50	*toast rounds or baked pie dough rounds*
½ cup	0.11 l	*oil*
50	50	*Italian plum tomatoes, slices, about 1 in. (25 mm) across*
1 cup	0.23 l	*pesto, purchased or recipe #R 170, page 74*
½ cup	0.11 l	*mustard seeds*

Scallops with mustard seeds recipe #H 212, this page.

Split scallops carefully in half and season with salt. Make sure scallops do not break. Place toast or pie rounds on oiled baking sheet, top with tomato, pesto and scallops. Brush with oil and put black mustard seeds in center. Bake at 500°F/275°C oven as needed. The scallops should not be cooked well done, but should be firm and crisp.

Scallop Croustade with Salsa   #H 213

Yield: 50 pieces

25	25	large scallops
½ tbsp	½ tbsp	salt
½ cup	0.11 l	oil
2 cups	0.46 l	salsa recipe #R 174, page 76
50	50	filo (cups) croustades (see filo nests, page 33)

Split scallops carefully in half and season with salt. Make sure scallops do not break. Sprinkle with oil. Bake at 500°F/275°C as needed. The scallops should not be cooked well done, but should be firm and crisp. Place 1 tsp salsa in each filo cup, put scallop on top. Serve at once.

#H 214

Sesame Scallops

Yield: 50 pieces

25	25	*large scallops*
½ cup	0.11 l	*white sesame seeds*
½ cup	0.11 l	*black sesame seeds*
½ tbsp	½ tbsp	*salt*
½ cup	0.11 l	*oil*
50	50	*toast rounds or pie dough rounds, baked*

Split scallops carefully in half and season with salt. Make sure scallops do not break. Blend sesame seeds. Dredge each scallop in seed mixture and place on oiled baking sheet. Sprinkle with oil. Bake at 500°F/275°C oven as needed. The scallops should not be cooked well done, but should be firm and crisp.

Note: Sesame seeds burn easily, so the baking process must be very short.

Sesame scallops recipe #H 214, this page.

Spicy Almonds

3	3	egg whites
½ cup	0.11 l	cold water
48 oz	1.35 kg	whole almonds, blanched
½ cup	0.11 l	coarse (kosher) salt
2 tbsp	2 tbsp	chili powder
1 tbsp	1 tbsp	oil

Mix egg whites and water, combine with almonds. Add salt and spices, mix well and lay on sheet pan to dry overnight. The next day mix with oil and bake in 400°F/200°C oven until light brown. Serve warm.

Note: Spices, such as curry, hot pepper or chili powder, and chopped herbs can be used in addition to salt. It is best to dry almonds overnight in a dry spot, such as on top of oven or in oven with only the pilot light on.

Tidbits with Blue Cheese, Walnuts, and Apples

blue cheese, apple, cream cheese, and walnut filling, recipe #R 130,
    page 55
rice paper
oil

Cut rice paper into 3 x 3 in. (75 x 75 mm) squares. Fill and put bundles or triangles on oiled baking sheet. Brush with oil and bake until bundles are brown and filling has melted, about 5 minutes. See directions on page 33.

#H 217   Zucchini, Tomato, and Mozzarella Silver Dollars

Yield: 50 pieces

50	50	*zucchini, slices, about 1¼ in. (32 mm) across and ¼ in. (7 mm) thick*
100	100	*cilantro leaves*
50	50	*Italian plum tomatoes, slices*
50	50	*mozzarella, slices, 1¼ in. (32mm) across*
½ cup	0.11 l	*olive oil*
		salt and pepper

Place zucchini slices on baking sheets, place cilantro leave on zucchini slice, followed by a tomato slice and one cheese slice. Brush with oil. Quickly broil as needed, but do not overcook. Serve these little sandwiches at once because they will get soggy when standing.

#H 218   Zucchini Rondelles with Shrimp

Yield: 50 pieces

4	4	*zucchini, about 7 in. (175 mm) long and about 1½ in. (37 mm) thick*
		shrimp filling recipe #R 143, page 61
		oil
		bread crumbs

Wash and cut zucchini in ¾ in. (18 mm) slices. Reserve end pieces, discard stems. Remove centers with a round ¾ in. (18 mm) cookie cutter. Chop zucchini pieces and add to shrimp mousse. Oil cookie sheet, sprinkle with bread crumbs, place zucchini rings on sheet, fill center heaped with shrimp mixture, sprinkle with bread crumbs. Bake in very hot oven until centers are solid, but zucchini slices are still crisp. Must be served right away because zucchini slices will dry out and filling will shrink.

Note: This item is difficult to eat when passed butler style.

Zucchini Rondelles with Fish Mousse   **#H 219**

Yield: 50 pieces

4	*4*	*zucchini, about 7 in. (175 mm) long and 1½ in. (37 mm) thick*
		fish mousse recipe #R 136, page 58
		oil
		bread crumbs

Follow directions for zucchini rings with shrimp on page 180. Use pastry bag to fill rings.

Zucchini Rondelles with Poultry Mousse   **#H 220**

Yield: 50 pieces

4	*4*	*zucchini, about 7 in. (175 mm) long and 1½ in. (37 mm) thick*
		poultry mousse #R 140, page 60
		oil
		bread crumbs

Follow directions for zucchini rings with shrimp on page 80. Use pastry bag to fill rings.

Barbecued, Broiled, and Grilled Items

Two plates with grilled items. Top plate is Anjou pears, barbecued recipe #H 221, this page; On bottom plate are broiled apricots with ham recipe #H 223, page 184; broiled prunes with blue cheese, recipe #H 224, page 184; and grilled polenta recipe #H 231, page 189.

#H 221

Barbecued Anjou Pears

Yield: 40

10	*10*	*Anjou pears, firm*
1½ cups	*0.34 l*	*barbecue sauce*
50	*50*	*wooden toothpicks*

Cut tops off pears about 1½ in. (37 mm) from top, cut the rest in quarters. Remove core. Brush with barbecue sauce and broil until brown. Serve with toothpicks.

Note: The pears should be firm. Apples can be used instead of pears.

The picture shows the assorted grilled vegetables mentioned in recipe #H 222, this page.

Grilled Baby Vegetables

#H 222

Yield: 50 pieces

> *50 pieces assorted baby vegetables such as asparagus, cauliflower, burdock, daikon, karela (bitter gourd), kohlrabi, red radishes, round eggplants, sweet green peppers, red peppers, turnips, tindora (Indian squash), zucchini, olive oil, salt, and pepper.*

Vegetables should be cut in bite-size pieces about the same size as vegetable crudité. Hard vegetables should be precooked before grilling. Burdock will take about 1 hour or longer boiling to become edible. It will turn brown in the process. Eggplant can become bitter and should be split and lightly salted about 2 hours before grilling to remove all bitterness. It should also be quickly parboiled. Karela is a bitter gourd and must be boiled in salted water with some tamarind paste to remove the bitterness.

The vegetables are mixed with olive oil and seasoned. They should be lightly grilled. They must not be very hot when served and should not be fatty.

Note: The concept is to present a warm crudité. Just about all vegetables can be grilled as long as they stay firm and crisp. Sauces or dips are not needed.

Broiled Apricots with Ham

Yield: 50 pieces

50	50	*large apricots*
50	50	*cooked ham, slices, 2 x 1 in. (50 x 25 mm)*
50	50	*wooden toothpicks*
		oil

Fasten ham to apricots with toothpicks. Brush with oil and broil until light brown.

Broiled Prunes with Blue Cheese

Yield: 50 pieces

12 oz	335 g	*blue cheese, crumbled*
4 oz	112 g	*cream cheese*
50	50	*large prunes, pitted*

Split prunes and with pastry bag fill with blue cheese. Broil until cheese is light brown.

Note: For butler style serve prunes on bread croustade. Spread croustade with cream cheese to prevent prunes from falling off.

Broiled Croustades of Salmon Tartare

#H 225

Yield: 60 pieces

24 oz	675 g	fresh salmon fillet
16 oz	450 g	smoked salmon
		salt and pepper
1 tbsp	1 tbsp	dill, chopped
		oil
60	60	baguette, slices, 1 in. (25 mm) across

Make sure all skin and bones are removed from salmon. Grind fresh and smoked salmon in meat grinder or chop coarsely in food processor. The mixture should not be too fine and smooth. Season with salt and pepper, and dill. With wet hands* form 60 patties. Place bread on baking sheet, brush with oil and toast on both sides. Place salmon patties on bread and broil in very hot oven, do not overcook.
* If patties are made ahead of time gloves should be used.

Broiled Shrimp Toast

#H 226

Yield: 100

shrimp spread recipe #R 143, page 61
bread

See directions on how to work with open sandwiches on page 36.

Three varieties of open sandwiches cut bite-size. Bottom and top: broiled shrimp toast recipe #H 226, this page. Right: broiled smoked salmon and fish mousse recipe #H 227, page 186. Left: broiled poultry mousse with sundried tomato pesto toast recipe #H 228, page 186.

#H 227

Broiled Smoked Salmon and Fish Mousse Toast

Yield: 100

		fish mousse recipe #R, 136 page 58
16 oz	450 g	*smoked salmon, sliced*
		rye bread

See directions on how to work with open sandwiches on page 36.

#H 228

Broiled Poultry Mousse Toast with Sun-dried Tomato Pesto

Yield: 50 pieces

		poultry mousse recipe #R 140, page 60
1 cup	0.23 l	*sun-dried tomato pesto*
		whole wheat bread

See directions on how to work with open sandwiches on page 36.

Deviled Beef

Yield: 50 pieces

1 cup	0.23 l	fresh mushrooms, chopped
½ cup	0.11 l	red wine
1 tsp	1 tsp	fresh thyme, chopped
1 tsp	1 tsp	butcher ground pepper
		salt to taste
1 cup	0.23 l	poultry mousse recipe #R 140, page 60
32 oz	900 g	roast beef, cooked, lean, well trimmed, sliced thin
⅔ cup	0.16 l	prepared mustard
2 cups	0.46 l	fresh bread crumbs
		oil

Make sure mushrooms are well washed before they are chopped. Combine mushrooms, red wine, thyme, and pepper. Bring mixture to boil and cook until all moisture is evaporated. Season with salt. Chill. Mix mushroom mixture with poultry mousse.

Make a beef "sandwich" by placing plastic kitchen wrap on table and arranging beef slices in a strip about 3 in. (75 mm) wide. Spread with mushroom-poultry mousse and cover again with beef slices. Wrap in plastic wrap and shape to a block about 3 in. (75 mm) wide and ½ in. (12 mm) thick. The length is immaterial. Continue making as many strips until all material is used up. Chill or freeze. Unwrap, trim and cut into pieces about 1½ in. (37 mm) x 1 in. (25 mm). Mix mustard with ½ cup (0.11 l) cold water and dredge pieces in mustard and bread crumbs. Sprinkle with oil and grill or broil until brown and the filling is cooked.

#H 230

Grilled Grave Lax

Yield: 50 pieces

1	1	salmon side, boneless, skin on, about 50 oz (1.40 kg), marinated according to grave lax recipe, page #R 178, page 78
1 cup	0.23 l	oil

Cut salmon into cubes, skin on. Place on baking sheet, skin up, brush with oil and broil until skin is crisp.

Note: Suitable for buffet.

On the platter are a variety of grilled items. Most noticeable are pieces of grilled grave lax recipe #H 230, this page. To the left and around are grilled salmon cubes wrapped with cucumbers recipe #H 233, page 190.

Grilled Polenta

Yield: 50 pieces

		polenta recipe #R 121, page 51
½ cup	0.11 l	oil

Cut polenta into bite-size squares or other convenient shapes. Brush with oil on both sides and brown on grill or griddle. Make sure items are not too hot when served.

Grilled Salmon with Roquefort and Capers

#H 232

Yield: 50 pieces

1 tbsp	1 tbsp	capers, drained
8 oz	225 g	Roquefort or Gorgonzola cheese
1	1	egg
¼ cup	0.06 l	sweet Sherry wine
50	50	fresh salmon, cubes, about 1 in. (25 mm) thick, skin removed
		rice wafer paper

Chop capers, combine with cheese, egg, and sherry, puree in food processor to fine paste. Cut rice wafer paper in squares about 4 x 4 in. (100 x 100 mm), place one salmon cube in center, top with 1 tsp filling. Wrap, oil, and grill lightly on both sides.

Note: Use pastry bag to put filling on fish. See page 37 for how to work with rice wafer paper.

#H 233

Grilled Salmon Cubes Wrapped with Cucumbers

Yield: 50 pieces

32 oz	*900 g*	*fresh salmon, skinless and boneless*
1 tbsp	*1 tbsp*	*salt*
4	*4*	*cucumbers, seedless hydroponic*
¼ cup	*0.06 l*	*salt*
1 cup	*0.23 l*	*oil*
50	*50*	*wooden toothpicks*

The best cuts of salmon to use are tail pieces. Salt salmon and refrigerate. Cut cucumbers in half and slice lengthwise on meat slicer into 50 thin slices. Use outside and end pieces for other recipes. Sprinkle slices with salt, let stand 30 minutes. Wrap each fish piece with one cucumber slice, secure with toothpick. Brush with oil and broil.

#H 234

Grilled Salsify (Oyster Plant)

Yield: 50 pieces

64 oz	*1.80 kg*	*salsify*
		juice of 2 lemons
		oil
		salt and pepper

Peel salsify and boil in water with lemon juice until tender, but not mushy. Brush with oil and grill. Season with salt and pepper to taste. Cut into 1 in. (25 mm) pieces.

Note: The item needs toothpicks when served butler style.

Grilled Shitake Mushrooms

Yield: 50 pieces

50	50	shitake mushrooms
¼ cup	0.06 l	olive oil
2 tbsp	2 tbsp	onions, chopped
1 cup	0.23 l	tomatoes, seeded and diced
2 tbsp	2 tbsp	balsamic vinegar
4 tbsp	4 tbsp	pesto, purchased or recipe #R 170, page 74
1 cup	0.23 l	Parmesan cheese, grated

Separate mushroom heads from stems and wash heads. Chop stems in food processor. Saute heads in 2 tbsp olive oil, set aside to cool. Saute onions in remaining oil, add mushroom stems and tomatoes. Saute over high heat until most moisture has evaporated. Add vinegar and pesto. Cool mixture. Fill mushroom heads with tomato mixture, sprinkle with grated cheese. Place on baking sheet and bake until warm and cheese has melted.

Note: Plates are needed for this item.

Grilled Swordfish Wrapped in Cucumbers

Yield: 50 pieces

32 oz	900 g	swordfish, center cut
¼ cup	0.06 l	paprika
¼ cup	0.06 l	oil
4	4	cucumbers, seedless hydroponic
¼ cup	0.06 l	salt
50	50	wooden toothpicks

Cut swordfish into 50 cubes, combine with paprika. Cut swordfish in half and slice lengthwise on meat slicer into 50 thin slices. Use outside and end pieces in other recipes. Sprinkle slices with salt, let stand 30 minutes. Wrap each fish piece with one cucumber slice, secure with toothpick. Brush with oil and broil.

#H 237   Grilled Tartare Steak

Yield: 50 pieces

48 oz	1.34 kg	ground beef round, very lean, very fresh
4	4	anchovy fillets
1 tbsp	1 tbsp	oil
1	1	egg
1 tbsp	1 tbsp	onions, chopped
1 tbsp	1 tbsp	capers, chopped
½ tbsp	½ tbsp	prepared mustard
½ tsp	½ tsp	pepper
50	50	baguette slices
		salt to taste

Make sure that meat is very fresh and finely ground. Chop anchovy, including oil, to fine puree. Combine all ingredients except bread. The mixture should be very tasty. Toast baguette slices on both sides. Cool. Spread meat mixture on each slice. Broil, meat side up, in very hot oven just until meat is brown, but not cooked. Serve immediately.

Note: There is concern about the safety of ground meat. The meat used in this dish must be very fresh, of best quality, and ground as close to service time as possible.

#H 238   Grilled Tuna Wrapped in Cucumbers

Follow directions for grilled swordfish, recipe #H 236, page 191, but replace with tuna. The tuna should be rare.

Grilled Tuna Roll and Daikon

#H 239

Yield: 50 pieces

6	6	daikon radishes, large
2 tbsp	2 tbsp	salt
50	50	fresh tuna, cut into strips 1½ in. (37 mm) long and ½ in. (12 mm) thick
3 tbsp	3 tbsp	sesame oil
¼ cup	0.06 l	oil
½ cup	0.11 l	soy sauce
50	50	wooden toothpicks

Peel radishes and slice lengthwise on meat slicer ⅛ in. (3 mm) thick. Trim slices to about 1 in. (25 mm) wide and 4 in. (100 mm) long. Add salt and let stand 10 minutes to make slices pliable. Roll tuna pieces with radish slices, secure with toothpicks. Blend remaining ingredients, pour over fish, and marinate 1 hour. Broil/bake in 500°F/275°C oven as needed. Tuna center should be rare.

Grilled Zucchini with Tofu

#H 240

Yield: 50 pieces

4	4	zucchini, about 2 in. (50 mm) in diameter
3 tbsp	3 tbsp	salt
3 tbsp	3 tbsp	sesame oil
25 oz	700 g	tofu, solid
¼ cup	0.06 l	oil
50	50	wooden toothpicks

Trim end off zucchini and wash. Slice zucchini lengthwise on slicer into thin, pliable strips. Marinate strips 1 hour with salt and sesame oil. Cut tofu in cubes. Wrap zucchini slices around tofu and secure with toothpicks. Brush with oil and grill lightly.

#H 241   ## Kibbeh (Lamb Meatballs)

Yield: 50 pieces

1 cup	0.23 l	bulgur wheat (cracked wheat)
3 cups	0.70 l	hot water
½ bunch	½ bunch	parsley
2 tbsp	2 tbsp	fresh mint, chopped
1	1	onion, medium
½ tbsp	½ tbsp	garlic, chopped
12 oz	338 g	lamb, ground, very lean
¼ tsp	¼ tsp	Tabasco sauce
½ tsp	½ tsp	allspice, ground
¼ tsp	¼ tsp	rosemary, ground
½ cup	0.11 l	pignoli (pine nuts)
1½ tbsp	1½ tbsp	salt

Combine bulgur and hot water. Soak for 10 minutes, drain, and cool. Chop parsley, mint, and onion very fine, combine with remaining ingredients. Shape patties and broil as needed.

#H 242   ## Salmon Sausage

Yield: 50 pieces

48 oz	1.34 kg	fresh salmon, skinned and all bones removed
4	4	egg whites
¼ cup	0.06 l	diced chives
2 tbsp	2 tbsp	fresh sage, chopped
2 tbsp	2 tbsp	salt
2 tbsp	2 tbsp	butcher ground pepper
		small sausage casing
		oil

Refrigerate egg whites about 30 minutes. Make sure salmon is very cold. Dice fish in small, ¼ in. (7 mm) cubes. Strain egg whites over salmon, add salt, chives, sage, and pepper, blend and mash ingredients. This is best done by hand (covered with a plastic glove). Salmon mixture should be coarse. Fill mixture in small sausage casings and poach about 25 minutes at 180°F/75°C. Let cool in stock. The sausage is coarse and rather dry because no fat has been added. Brush with oil and grill lightly.

Fried Items

Camembert fritters recipe #H 243, this page, and Parmesan and Swiss cheese pearls recipe #H 256, page 203, coming off the fryer.

Camembert or Brie Cheese Fritter

#H 243

Yield: 50 pieces

1 cup	0.23 l	milk
6 oz	170 g	flour
2 oz	56 g	butter
¼ tsp	¼ tsp	nutmeg
¼ tsp	¼ tsp	white pepper, ground
2	2	eggs
16 oz	450 g	Camembert or Brie cheese, ripe and soft
		cayenne pepper
		salt and pepper to taste
		breading
		oil for frying

Combine milk, flour, butter, and spices in saucepan, mix with whisk and then with wooden paddle. Bring to boil and cook until paste is thick and longer sticks to sides of pot. Pour paste into food processor. Add eggs and cheese, mix well. Spread mixture on oiled sheet pan to cool. Shape with wet hands or with small scoop into small croquettes. Bread and fry.

#H 244

Crayfish and Crabmeat Pearls

Yield: 100 pieces

1½ cups	0.34 l	crayfish tails, cooked and shelled
1½ cups	0.34 l	Alaskan crabmeat, defrosted
3 tbsp	3 tbsp	Spanish paprika
1 tbsp	1 tbsp	crab seasoning
		cream puff paste recipe #R 107, page 44
		oil for frying

Coarsely chop crayfish tails and crabmeat. Add all ingredients to cream puff paste. Shape small dumplings with scoop and fry in oil until brown and fully cooked through.

Note: Fritters will take a while to bake through. They will split before completely cooked. Check frequently.

Crayfish and crabmeat pearls recipe #H 244, this page. Whole crayfish are used as decoration and to indicate the flavor of the items presented.

Cream Puff Pearls with Pesto

#H 245

Yield: 100 pieces

1 cup	0.34 l	pesto
½ cup	0.11 l	spinach, cooked, well drained, ground
½ cup	0.11 l	cheese, grated
		cream puff paste recipe #R 107, page 44
		oil for frying

Add all ingredients to cream puff paste. Shape small dumplings with scoop and fry in oil until brown and fully cooked through.

Note: Pesto is best purchased ready to use or refer to recipe #R 170, page 74.

Note: Fritters will take a while to bake through. They will split before completely cooked. Check frequently.

Fried Gruyère Cheese

#H 246

Yield: 50 pieces

4 oz	112 g	flour
1½ oz	40 g	rice flour
16 oz	0.46 l	milk
3	3	eggs
2	2	egg yolks
1 tsp	1 tsp	nutmeg
		salt to taste
1 cup	0.23 l	Gruyère cheese, diced small

Combine first three ingredients, mix with wire whisk. Bring to boil, stirring continuously with wooden spoon, cook until mixture is very thick. Take off heat, add eggs, nutmeg, and salt, mix well. Add cheese. Spread mixture on oiled baking sheet, cover with foil and refrigerate. When cold cut into squares or rounds. Dip in batter or bread. Fry until brown.

#H 247 ## Fried Ginger Chips

Yield: 50 pieces

12 oz	338 g	*fresh ginger*
		tempura batter recipe #R 112, page 47
		oil for frying

Peel ginger and slice into ⅛ in. (3 mm) disks. Dip in batter and fry.

Note: Ginger is rather sharp and some customers might not enjoy it.

#H 248 ## Fried Grapes

Yield: 50 pieces

64 oz	1.80 kg	*seedless grapes*
		flour
		egg wash
		fresh bread crumbs
		oil for frying

Separate grapes into small clusters, about 4–5 grapes on each. Wash and drain. Carefully bread with flour, egg wash and bread crumbs. Deep-fry until golden brown.

#H 249 ## Fried Mozzarella

Yield: 50 pieces

48 oz	1.34 kg	*mozzarella cheese*
		cream cheese dough recipe #HT 101, page 29
		egg wash
		oil for frying

Cut cheese in pieces about 1½ in. (37 mm) long and ½ in. (12 mm) thick. Roll dough on pastry board, cut into ½ in. (12 mm) strips, paint with egg wash and wrap dough around cheese. Quickly fry pieces until light brown. Serve at once.

Note: Painting the dough will make it adhere better to the cheese. The item can be made ahead and refrigerated, but not frozen. However, it must be fried at the last moment.

Fried Leaves and Herbs

spinach leaves, sage leaves, curly parsley, red Swiss chard leaves,
  rosemary
oil

A number of leaves can be fried and the items mentioned above work rather well. Wash, drain well. Deep-fry until crisp, but not brown. Dry on paper towel and keep warm to dry out.

Note: The product is somewhat crumbly, but if carefully made it can be picked up without breaking into pieces. This is a specialty item and not suitable for large groups, but can be fun at a small buffet.

Silver platter with assorted fried leaves and herbs as described in recipe #H 250, this page.

#H 251

Fried Plantain Slices

Yield: 50 pieces

50	50	*plantain slices, about ⅛ in. (3 mm) thick*
½ cup	0.11 l	*dry barbecue spice*
¼ cup	0.06 l	*lemon juice*
		flour
		egg wash
		cornmeal
		oil for frying

Plantains should be ripe (yellow) but not mushy. Sprinkle barbecue spice and lemon juice over banana slices, mix well. Carefully bread with flour, egg wash and cornmeal. Deep-fry until golden brown.

Note: The same dish can be made with firm bananas.

#H 252

Fried Walnuts

48 oz	1.35 kg	*walnut halves, shelled*
8 oz	225 g	*sugar*
½ cup	0.11 l	*water*
½ cup	0.11 l	*molasses*
½ cup	0.11 l	*salt*
4 tbsp	4 tbsp	*pepper*
		oil for frying

Combine water and sugar in large pot, melt and cook until brown to caramel stage. Add molasses, stir well and add walnuts. Roast over fire until walnuts are evenly coated. Add salt and pepper, stir, and spread on sheet pan to dry. Fry walnuts in hot oil until crisp and brown as needed.

Note: Walnuts will brown fast because of a high sugar level. Frying oil will deteriorate quickly because of the spices and sugar. For this reason, walnuts should be fried in a small quantity of oil and not in a fryer used for other foods.

Fried Baby Zucchini

Yield: 100 pieces

50 each	*50 each*	*whole baby zucchini*
		flour
		egg wash
		fresh bread crumbs
		oil for frying

Wash and trim zucchini, split lengthwise if thick. Dry. Bread and fry until golden brown.

Fried baby zucchini recipe #H 253, this page.

#H 254

Lobster and Shrimp Cream Puff Pearls

Yield: 100 pieces

16 oz	450 g	lobsters (2 each)
16 oz	450 g	raw shrimp, any size
¼ cup	0.06 l	oil
1 tbsp	1 tbsp	tomato puree
1 pinch	1 pinch	cayenne pepper
½ tsp	½ tsp	fresh tarragon, chopped
1 tbsp	1 tbsp	paprika
		salt to taste
1 cup	0.23 l	white wine
32 oz	0.92 l	lobster or shrimp stock
		cream puff paste recipe #R 107, page 44, modified
		oil for frying

Split lobster, remove tail and tamale. Peel and devein shrimp. Saute lobster shells and shrimp shells in oil over slow heat. Add spices, wine, tomato puree and 32 oz (0.92 l) water. Bring to boil and simmer 1 hour. Strain, save stock, discard shells. Make cream puff paste according to recipe, substituting shellfish stock for milk. Chop lobster meat, tamale, and shrimp in food processor. Add to cooled cream puff paste. Form fritters with scoop # 24 and bake in hot oil until brown.

Note: Fritters will take a while to bake through. They will split before completely cooked. Check frequently.

#H 255

Lotus Root Tempura

Yield: Dependent upon size

lotus root
tempura batter recipe #R 112, page 47

Peel fresh lotus root, cut in ⅛ in. (3 mm) slices, soak 1 hour in cold water. Boil roots in water 1 hour, let cool in stock. Drain, dip in tempura batter and fry. The slices look very attractive. Serve with a ginger dip recipe #R 171, page 75.

Parmesan and Swiss Cheese Pearls #H 256

Yield: 100 pieces

2 cups	0.46 l	Parmesan cheese, grated
1 cup	0.23 l	Swiss cheese, cut in very small dice
		cream puff paste recipe #R 107, page 47
		oil for frying

Add all ingredients to lukewarm cream puff paste. Shape small dumplings with scoop and fry in oil until brown and fully cooked through.

Note: Fritters will take a while to cook through. They will split before completely cooked. Check frequently. Do not add Swiss cheese to hot cream puff paste because the mixture can become stringy.

Potato Napoleon with Caviar and Sour Cream #H 257

Yield: 50 pieces

1 cup	0.23 l	sour cream
4 tbsp	4 tbsp	diced chives
14	14	Russet potatoes, 100 size
1 cup	0.23 l	salmon caviar
1 cup	0.23 l	black caviar
		oil for frying

Combine sour cream and chives, keep refrigerated. Peel potatoes. Wash and trim to cylindrical shape 1¼ in. (32 mm) across. Slice cylinders on meat slicer or mandolin into very thin slices, about 1/16 in. (2 mm) thick. 150 slices are required. Soak 1 hour and wash well in cold water. Remove to drain. Heat frying oil to 400°F/200°C and carefully fry potatoes in small patches until cooked, light brown but not crisp. Drain and keep warm. Assemble circles in stacks consisting of one slice potato, topped with sour cream and red caviar, the next slice with sour cream and black caviar, topped with the third slice.

Note: The quality of caviar determines the flavors of the dish. If excellent black caviar is not available it is better to use only salmon caviar. Frying the potato chips requires care, they should not be limp but slightly crisp. If they are too crisp the items is difficult to eat. Assembly must be at the last moment, the combination of warm potatoes and cold filling is pleasing.

#H 258

Quail Scots Eggs

Yield: 50

50	50	*quail eggs*
2 tbsp	2 tbsp	*chopped parsley*
		poultry stuffing recipe #R 140, page 60
		flour
4	4	*eggs*
		bread crumbs
		oil for frying

Boil eggs for 3 minutes, chill. Carefully peel eggs in cold water. The center should still be soft and moist. Place eggs on towel to dry. Combine parsley with poultry stuffing. Roll quail eggs in flour and carefully coat each quail egg with poultry mousse. This is best done with wet hands and can be time-consuming. Chill eggs until very firm. Roll eggs in flour and bread with egg wash and fresh bread crumbs. Deep-fry in oil until brown.

Quail Scots eggs recipe #H 258, this page, ready to be passed butler style. The platter is garnished with a nest of hard-boiled quail eggs, which were later used for canapes. Boiling the eggs avoids problems if a customer or employee drops one.

Rice Paper Fritters

Most fillings can be wrapped in double layers of rice paper and deep-fried. Breading is not needed. If the filling is very wet or will melt during frying, the products should be wrapped twice with double layers. Like all rice paper wrapped items it is advisable to chill/freeze the product before frying.

Roquefort Fritters with Honey   #H 260

Yield: 50 pieces

½ cup	0.11 l	walnuts, chopped
16 oz	450 g	Roquefort cheese
16 oz	450 g	cream cheese
2	2	eggs
½ cup	0.11 l	fresh, soft bread crumbs
2 tbsp	2 tbsp	honey
		rice wafer paper
		frying batter with beer
		recipe #R 111, page 46
		oil for frying

Toast walnuts. In food processor combine cheese, eggs, bread crumbs and honey. Blend in nuts. Place about ½ tbsp mixture on rice wafer paper, fold into neat bundles. Place on oiled sheet pan. Refrigerate or freeze. Dip in frying batter and fry.

#H 261

Scallop Napoleon with Basil

Yield: 50 pieces

1	1	egg
½ cup	0.11 l	heavy cream
		filo dough, recipe #HT 102, page 32
50	50	fresh basil leaves
25	25	sea scallops
½ cup	0.11 l	pesto purchased or recipe #R 170, page 74
½ cup	0.11 l	prepared very thick cream sauce
		oil for frying

Combine egg and heavy cream. Place double layers filo sheets on pastry board and cut with cookie cutter into 1½ in. (37 mm) circles. Brush rim with egg mixture and place small basil leaf in center. Cover with second filo circle, press edges together. Make 50 circles with and 50 circles without basil center for the bottom. Fry quickly until golden brown. Keep warm. Cut scallops horizontally in half, brush with oil and place on baking sheet. Combine pesto and cream sauce, it should be a thick mixture. As

Scallop Napoleon with basil recipe #H 261, this page.

needed, quickly broil scallops under high heat until brown but still moist, place a dab of pesto sauce on each filo bottom, put a scallop on top, put a little pesto on the scallop and cover with the top filo piece.

Note: The pesto sauce must be thick and acts as flavor enhancer and adhesive to keep the pieces together. Filo dough is hard to work with and it is quicker to make squares than circles. However, scallops are round and circles look better. The circles can also be brushed with oil and baked. The item is fun, but very labor-intensive and difficult to eat.

Sweet Potato Napoleon with Smoked Salmon   **#H 262**

Yield: 50 pieces

The same ingredients as in recipe #H 257, page 203, but substitute sweet potatoes for Russet potatoes and sliced smoked salmon for caviar.

    Peel sweet potatoes and cut into rounds about 1¼ in. (32 mm) across and about ¹⁄₁₆ in. (2 mm) thick. 100 slices are required. Cover with water, bring to boil and drain immediately. Spread on sheet pan to dry. Fry carefully until crisp and light brown. Note that sweet potatoes will brown fast because of the high sugar content.

Surimi (Imitation Crabmeat) Cream Puff Pearls   **#H 263**

Follow the recipe #H 244, page 196, but replace crayfish and crabmeat with surimi.

Potato chips with sage, marjoram, and oregano.

#H 264

Transparent Potato Chips with Herbs

Russet potatoes
fresh herbs
egg whites
oil for frying

Peel potatoes and slice lengthwise about 1/16 in. (2 mm) thick. Do not put in water. With oval cookie cutter, cut disks. Put a sprig of fresh herbs between two potato slices, brush rim lightly with egg white, and press together like a sandwich. Deep-fry until transparent and crisp. Dry on paper towel to remove excess oil.

Note: The chips cannot be fried until completely crisp because it is important to show the herbs in the center. The product must be dried in a warm oven until crisp. Transparent chips are a fun but labor-intensive novelty.

Vegetable Tempura

Yield: Dependent upon vegetable used

> *vegetables cut in bite-size strips*
> *tempura batter, recipe #R 112 page 47*
> *oil for frying.*
> *dipping sauce*

Basically all vegetables can be fried, such as red, green, and yellow peppers, mushrooms, Swiss chard stems and leaves, scallions, radishes, cauliflower, broccoli, red onions, parsley, asparagus, snow peas, sugar snap peas. Dip vegetables one by one in batter and fry until light brown. Batter is thin and the vegetables will show through. Spread vegetables to dry on absorbent paper, do not pile vegetables on top of each other to prevent getting soft. Serve as soon as possible. Traditionally a soy sauce variety is served with tempura. This can become messy in butler service and the vegetables are delicious without sauce.

International Items

Oriental

#H 266

Glazed Scallops

Yield: 50 pieces

50	50	sea scallops, medium (bite-size)
1½ cups	0.34 l	mirin
1½ cups	0.34 l	soy sauce
		oil

Wash scallops, drain, and marinate in mirin about one hour. Drain and save marinade. Combine marinade with soy sauce and reduce to about half. Place scallops on suitable broiler pan, brush with oil and sauce. Broil at high heat, turn, brush with sauce, and broil on the other side. Scallops should be underdone in the center and should not be burned.

#H 267

Harusame Shrimp Tempura

Yield: 50 pieces

50	50	shrimp, 24/24 size, peeled and deveined
		juice of 2 lemons
		frying batter recipe #R 113, page 47
10 oz	280 g	harusame noodles, crushed
		oil for frying

Marinate shrimp in lemon juice. Add tempura batter to shrimp, mix well. If mixture seems too liquid add a little flour. Dip each shrimp in crushed noodles and fry. Noodles will expand, do not overcrowd fryer. Do not brown noodles too much.

Rolled Egg Omelette with Tuna and Rice   #H 268

Yield: 50 pieces

¼ cup	0.06 l	soy sauce
¼ cup	0.06 l	mirin
24 oz	670 g	fresh tuna, trimmed
1 tbsp	1 tbsp	oil
12	12	eggs
2 tbsp	2 tbsp	water
1 bunch	1 bunch	scallions
1 cup	0.23 l	sushi rice, cooked, recipe #R 126, page 53

Combine soy sauce and mirin. Cut tuna into strips about ¾ in. (18 mm) thick and as long as possible. Marinate overnight in soy mixture. Sear tuna on broiler or pan, the fish should still be medium rare in center. Combine eggs with water. Make very thin omelettes by pouring just enough mixture into a nonstick frying pan to cover bottom. Cook over low heat on one side until mixture is set. Place pancakes on table to cool. Clean scallions, only green part will be used. Place tuna strips, scallions, and rice on pancakes, roll into tight roll, place seam side down on baking sheet. Cover with foil. Warm as needed and slice into 1 in. (25 mm) pieces.

Note: Use sensible sanitary precautions because undercooked fish will spoil rapidly if exposed to warm temperatures. The dish is best assembled just before service.

Smoked Salmon Nori Roll   #H 269

Yield: 50 pieces

10	10	Nori (seaweed), sheets
16 oz	450 g	smoked salmon, sliced
1	1	cucumber, seedless
½ cup	0.11 l	wasabe
		sushi rice, cooked, recipe #R 126, page 53
		oil

Make rolls with Nori, salmon, peeled cucumber strips, wasabe, and rice. Roll up tightly and refrigerate. Cut rolls into 1 in. (25 mm) pieces, place on baking sheet with rice facing up, brush with oil, and bake in very hot oven until hot.

Note: Nori should be toasted over an open flame to improve flavor.

#H 270

Teryaki Beef Tidbits

Yield: 50 pieces

2 tbsp	2 tbsp	oil
32 oz	900 g	beef tenderloin/sirloin or top sirloin tidbits
¼ cup	0.06 l	dark soy sauce
¼ cup	0.06 l	mirin
¼ cup	0.06 l	sake
¼ tsp	¼ tsp	garlic, chopped
¼ cup	0.06 l	scallions, chopped

Heat oil and saute meat a few minutes, add all other ingredients. Cook over high heat and stir until most liquid is evaporated and the meat is nicely glazed. Serve with toothpicks.

#H 271

Teryaki Glazed Beef Rolls

Yield: 50 pieces

¼ cup	0.06 l	dark soy sauce
¼ cup	0.06 l	mirin
¼ cup	0.06 l	sake
¼ tsp	¼ tsp	garlic, chopped
¼ cup	0.06 l	scallions, chopped
1 tbsp	1 tbsp	sugar
10	10	beef sirloin raw, very thin slices
10	10	scallions
2 tbsp	2 tbsp	oil

Combine marinade ingredients. Make sure beef is cut very thin, trim off all fat and gristle. Each slice should measure about 2 x 5 in. (50 x 125 mm). Clean scallion and cut into 5 in. (125 mm) center cut pieces. Roll each slice lengthwise around scallion and secure with toothpicks. Place in marinade for 1 hour. Saute meat in oil, add marinade and let reduce, turning meat frequently to glaze evenly. For service remove toothpicks and slice into 1 in. (25 mm) slices.

*Steamed seafood dumplings recipe
#H 272, this page.*

Wontons can be shaped as the picture indicates. It takes much practice to make the shapes quickly and efficiently. Many ready to use products are on the market. Wontons can be filled with many fillings and steamed or fried.

Note: Wonton skins are best purchased ready to use. They are available plain and with eggs, both in different sizes, round and square. The recipe for wonton skins is #R 128, page 54.

Steamed Seafood Dumplings #H 272

Yield: 50 pieces

		seafood filling recipe #R 142, page 61
50	50	round wonton skins
2½ tbsp	2½ tbsp	flour
½ cup	0.11 l	cold water

Mix flour with cold water. Place 1½ tsp filling in center of each wonton skin, brush edges with flour mixture and shape dumplings. Steam 15 minutes.

Note: Dumplings with different fillings are available ready to steam or to fry from a number of manufacturers. It takes much skill to shape to dumplings rapidly and evenly.

#H 273   # Steamed Dumplings with Pork

Yield: 50 pieces

2½ tbsp	2½ tbsp	*flour*
½ cup	0.11 l	*cold water*
		pork filling with anise recipe #R 139, page 59
50	50	*round wonton skins*

Mix flour with cold water. Place 1½ tsp filling in center, brush edges with flour mixture and shape dumplings. Steam 15 minutes. Cover with moist towel until service. Serve with soy dip.

Note: Dumplings with different fillings are available ready to steam or to fry from a number of manufacturers. It takes much skill to shape to dumplings rapidly and evenly.

#H 274   # Egg Rolls

Yield: 150 pieces

1 tbsp	1 tbsp	*oil*
1 tbsp	1 tbsp	*fresh ginger, chopped*
3 tbsp	3 tbsp	*scallions, chopped (greens included)*
16 oz	450 g	*pork or pork sausage, ground*
1 cup	0.23 l	*bean sprouts, chopped coarsely*
1 cup	0.23 l	*bok choy (Chinese cab bage) coarsely, chopped*
¼ cup	0.06 l	*water chestnuts, chopped*
16 oz	450 g	*shrimp, raw, broken pieces*
1 tbsp	1 tbsp	*sesame oil*
¼ cup	0.06 l	*soy sauce*
1 tbsp	1 tbsp	*sugar*
		salt and pepper to taste
1 tbsp	1 tbsp	*cornstarch*
150	150	*square wonton skins, 3 x 3 in. (75 x 75 mm)*
2½ tbsp	2½ tbsp	*flour*
½ cup	0.11 l	*cold water*

In wide, shallow pan or wok saute in oil ginger and scallions until wilted. Add pork and fry until brown and crumbly; frequent stirring is necessary to break up pieces. Add vegetables and cook over high heat until most water is evaporated. Add shrimp and remaining ingredients except cornstarch, wonton skins, flour, and water. Mix cornstarch with 1½ tbsp cold water and add to filling, bring to boil, check seasoning and cool. The mixture should be moist, but not wet. Mix flour and water for sealing paste. Fill wrappers with about 1½ tbsp filling, make rolls, and seal edges with paste. Fry until golden brown. Serve with soy sauce.

Note: Frozen egg rolls are available in many sizes and with different fillings.

South of the border

#H 275

Colombian Empanadas

Yield: 50 pieces

> *empanada blue corn dough recipe #R 108, page 45*
> *empanada filling recipe #R 135, page 57*

Form half moon shaped turnovers with empanada dough, fill, close tightly, and refrigerate. Empanadas can be baked or fried.

#H 276

Mexican Empanadas

Yield: 60 pieces

> *empanada masa harina dough recipe #R 110, page 46*
> *beef filling for empanada recipe #R 129, page 54*

Form half moon shaped turnovers with empanada dough, fill, close tightly, and refrigerate. Empanadas can be baked or fried.

#H 277

Baked Platanos (Plantains)

Yield: 50 pieces

64 oz	1.80 kg	*ripe plantains*
2 tbsp	2 tbsp	*coarse (kosher) salt*
½ cup	0.11 l	*oil*

Peel plantains and cut into bite-size pieces. Sprinkle with salt and oil and bake at 375°F/190°C until cooked.

Note: Product must be served with toothpicks and a suitable dip such as tomatillo dip, recipe #R 176, page 77, or recipe #R 168, page 73, green lime dip.

*Refried beans pasa bocas recipe
#H 278, this page.*

Refried Bean Pasa Bocas

#H 278

Yield: 48

3 cups	0.70 l	refried beans, canned or homemade
½ tbsp	½ tbsp	mole powder
8	8	flour tortillas, 8 in. (200 mm)
1 cup	0.23 l	fresh bread crumbs
1	1	egg white
		oil

Mix beans with mole powder and 1 cup (0.23 l) bread crumbs. Spread tortillas with bean mixture, roll up tightly. Cover and freeze for 1 hour. Cut into bite-size pieces. Mix egg white with 1 tbsp cold water. Dip ends of tortilla pieces in egg white and then in bread crumbs to seal. Place pieces on baking sheet, seam down. Brush with oil and bake until hot and crisp.

Note: The tortillas are easier to handle when slightly frozen.

#H 279

Refried Bean Pizza

Yield: 50 pieces

16 oz	450 g	sausage meat
2 cups	0.46 l	canned or reconstituted refried beans
½ tbsp	½ tbsp	chili powder
50	50	flaky yeast dough, #HT 103, page 34, rounds, 1½ in. (37 mm) across
2 cups	0.46 l	mozzarella cheese or queso blanco, shredded

Cook sausage meat slowly until brown and crumbly. Frequent stirring is necessary to break up pieces. Drain off most fat. Add beans and chili powder, heat. Cool mixture to room temperature. Top dough rounds with bean mixture, then with cheese, and bake until brown and crisp.

Note: Bean mixture is best applied with a pastry bag on frozen dough rounds. Refried beans are available canned and dehydrated.

#H 280

Tamales with Corn Masa and Beef

Tamales are steamed stuffed leaves, normally cornhusks or palm leaves. However, they are not edible. For our purpose we substitute leaves with rice wafer paper and the item becomes completely edible.

Yield: 75 pieces

¼ cup	0.06 l	lard
2 cups	0.46 l	masa harina
1¼ cups	0.06 l	warm water
½ tsp	½ tsp	salt
		rice wafer paper
		beef filling recipe #R 129, page 54
		oil

Melt lard and blend with remaining ingredients except beef filling. Let mixture rest 1 hour before use. Fill rice wafer paper. Brush with oil and steam 15 minutes. Let rest before service.

Note: For directions on how to work with rice wafer paper see page 36. The item can be made ahead and chilled or frozen before it is steamed.

Tamales with Corn Masa and Chicken #H 281

Yield: 50 pieces

		Jalapeño pepper to taste
¼ cup	0.06 l	*lard*
10 oz	280 g	*masa harina*
4 cups	0.92 l	*hot water*
½ tsp	½ tsp	*salt*
½ tsp	½ tsp	*cumin powder*
		rice wafer paper
1 cup	0.23 l	*chicken, cooked and diced*
		oil

Remove seeds from Jalapeño peppers and cut into small dice. Melt lard and blend with remaining ingredients except chicken. Let mixture rest 1 hour before use. Fill rice wafer paper with masa and chicken. Brush with oil and steam 15 minutes. Let rest before service.

Note: The amount of Jalapeño pepper depends on season and on the ripeness of the peppers. Some are very hot and should be used with great caution. For directions how to work with rice wafer paper see page 36. The item can be made ahead and chilled or frozen before it is steamed.

Tartlets with Turkey and Mole #H 282

Yield: 50

		turkey mole filling recipe
		#R 164, page 71
50	50	*baked tartlet shells dough*
		recipe #HT 104, page 35

Fill tartlets as needed with hot mixture.

Vegetable Empanadas #H 283

Yield: 50 pieces

empanada blue corn dough recipe #R 108, page 45, or #R 109, page 46, or #R 110, page 46
vegetable filling recipe #R 147, page 63

Form half moon shaped turnovers with empanada dough, fill, close tightly, and refrigerate. Empanadas can be baked or fried.

India

Bombay Duck

*Bombay duck
oil for frying*

Bombay duck is dried fish, sold in boneless fillets about 4 in. (100 mm) long. The fillets are deep-fried or toasted until crisp. Break into bite-size pieces. The product is very salty and should be served with other foods.

Note: The product has a strong smell when being cooked. This smell will disappear after a little while, but is not recommended to use this product for off premise catering.

Chapati (vegetarian)

Indian flat, soft bread, served warm. The basic dough is flavorless, but can be seasoned with curry, turmeric, cumin, and peppers. The bread is served warm, cut in half, and can be served with a vegetarian dip or yoghurt dip.

Yield: 15 pieces

1¾ cups	0.41 l	chapati flour
¾ cup	0.17 l	water

Combine ingredients to soft dough. Cover and let rest for ½ hour. On pastry board shape into 15 balls. Roll into 5 in. (125 mm) circles with rolling pin. Fry on hot griddle until puffed up and light brown on both sides. Cut in quarters and serve warm.

Note: Chapatis are often served with a dip.

Falafel (Chickpea Fritter) (vegetarian) #H 286

Yield: 100 pieces

1 #10 can	1 #10 can	cooked chickpeas (gar-banzos)
1 cup	0.23 l	flour
4	4	eggs
1 tsp	1 tsp	cumin
		salt and pepper
		oil for frying

Drain chickpeas. There should be about 72 oz (2 kg) drained product. Process to coarse puree in food processor. Add other ingredients to make stiff batter. Drop small fritters on oiled nonstick frying pan and cook on both sides.

Note: The amount of flour needed varies according to moisture content of chickpeas puree. Ready-to-use falafel mix is available.

Gobhi Pakode (Coriander Flavored Cauliflower Fritters) #H 287

Yield: 125 pieces

		basic falafel batter, as in recipe #H 286, page 221
1 tbsp	1 tbsp	coriander seeds, crushed
2 tbsp	2 tbsp	oil
2 cups	0.46 l	cauliflower florets, raw
		oil for frying

Make batter and add coriander, oil, and cauliflower. Let batter rest 1 hour in warm place. Drop small fritters on hot griddle.

Note: Coriander seeds improve in flavor if toasted lightly before use.

#H 288 Jheenga Pakode (Shrimp Fritters)

Yield: 50 pieces

40 oz	1.12 kg	shrimp, 20/24 size
1 tsp	1 tsp	garlic, crushed with 1 tsp salt
1 tbsp	1 tbsp	ginger, chopped
2 cups	0.46 l	chickpeas, cooked and drained
1 cup	0.23 l	flour
2	2	eggs
1 cup	0.23 l	buttermilk
1 tbsp	1 tbsp	curry powder or masala paste
		cayenne pepper to taste
		salt to taste
		oil for frying

Peel shrimp but leave tail on. Mix with garlic and ginger, set aside 1 hour. Process chickpeas to puree in food processor. Add flour, eggs, buttermilk and spices to make stiff batter. Dip shrimp in batter and deep-fry.

Note: The amount of flour varies depending on the moisture content of the chickpea puree.

#H 289 Pakorhas (Vegetable Fritters Made with Besan)

Yield: 60 pieces

1½ cups	0.34 l	besan (chickpea flour)
1 tsp	1 tsp	masala paste
¼ tsp	¼ tsp	garlic, crushed with 1 tsp salt
¼ tsp	¼ tsp	turmeric
¼ tsp	¼ tsp	chili powder
1 cup	0.23 l	water
1 cup	0.23 l	raw broccoli, chopped
1 cup	0.23 l	raw cauliflower, chopped
1 cup	0.23 l	raw celery, chopped
½ cup	0.11 l	raw red peppers, chopped
½ cup	0.11 l	scallions, chopped
		oil for frying

Combine ingredients except vegetables to thick paste in food processor. Let rest in warm place about 1 hour. Add the vegetables. Fry small fritters on griddle or drop in oil.

Udad or Papadoms

#H 290

1 pkg udad
oil for frying

Udad is an Indian bread, available in dried disks about 6 in. (150 mm) across. Many flavors are available and some can be very hot. The disks are fried quickly, one disk at a time, in oil, drained, and served warm. The customers are expected to break off little pieces.

Note: The item is an inexpensive and interesting snack for bars.

Basket with assorted Papadoms.

Pan- and Griddle-fried Items

Pancakes and fritters

#H 291   Arugula Fritters (vegetarian)

Yield: 60/70

2 cups	0.46 l	arugula, chopped
3 cups	0.70 l	fresh spinach, chopped
1 cup	0.23 l	romaine lettuce, chopped
½ tsp	½ tsp	garlic, chopped
3	3	eggs
½ cup	0.11 l	cake flour
1 tsp	1 tsp	coarse black pepper
		salt to taste
		oil

Make sure greens are well washed, especially arugula because it is often sandy. Place in sauce pot, add garlic and pepper. Cover and steam until soft, about 15 minutes. Cool, but do not drain. Add salt to taste, eggs, and flour. Mixture should have consistency of pancake batter. If needed, more flour should be added, or excess cooking liquid drained off. With tablespoon drop small fritters on oiled griddle or nonstick pan, flatten slightly, cook on both sides.

Note: Arugula is a strong tasting, bitter salad green. By adding spinach and lettuce the flavor is softened, but the fritter is still rather strong tasting. It should appeal to vegetarians.

Bean Cakes

Yield: 120 cakes

1 #10 can	1 #10 can	refried beans, about 13 cups (2.8 l)
1 tbsp	1 tbsp	cumin powder
½ tsp	½ tsp	hot pepper
3	3	eggs
		fresh bread crumbs as needed
		cornmeal
		oil

Blend beans with spices and eggs in food processor. Add bread crumbs to make a stiff mixture which can be shaped into patties. Shape patties with ice cream scoop # 24, dredge in cornmeal and griddle fry.

Note: Beans must be of good quality. If product is not tasty it can be improved by adding crumbled bacon bits. Refried beans are available canned or dehydrated.

Black Bean and Chili Burger

Yield: 100

6 cups	1.40 l	refried beans
32 oz	900 g	ground beef, lean
1 tbsp	1 tbsp	chili powder
½ tsp	½ tsp	hot pepper
2 tbsp	2 tbsp	cilantro (coriander leaves), chopped
2 tbsp	2 tbsp	parsley, chopped
		salt to taste
1 cup	0.23 l	cold water
		fresh bread crumbs as needed
		cornmeal
		oil

Blend beans, meat, spices, and water in food processor. Add bread crumbs to make mixture stiff enough to shape into patties. Make patties with ice cream scoop # 24, dredge in cornmeal and griddle fry.

Note: The patties should be flattened out to cook evenly and should be cooked well done.

#H 294

Black-eyed Peas Fritters

Yield: 50 pieces

2 cups	0.46 l	black-eyed peas, dried
¼ tsp	¼ tsp	hot red pepper
½ tsp	½ tsp	fennel seeds, chopped
2 tbsp	2 tbsp	onions, chopped
1 tsp	1 tsp	salt
2	2	eggs
3 tbsp	3 tbsp	flour
		oil

Soak peas in cold water until skins slip off, about 1 hour. Rub peas together to remove skins; they will float on top. Remove skins. Boil peas until soft. Drain and puree peas in food processor. Add remaining ingredients. Drop little fritters on hot griddle or into a nonstick frying pan.

Note: Depending on moisture content of the cooked peas some water might have to be added to the batter.

#H 295

Broccoli Fritters (vegetarian)

Yield: 50 pieces

48 oz	1.34 kg	fresh broccoli
4	4	eggs
1 cup	0.23 l	fresh bread crumbs
1 tsp	1 tsp	savory, chopped
¼ tsp	¼ tsp	nutmeg
		salt and pepper

Remove leaves from broccoli. Cut off stems and peel. Cut stems in thin slices. Steam flowers and stems separately until both are tender, but not overcooked. Cool and puree. The puree should be rather dry. Mix with eggs, bread crumbs, and seasoning. Make small fritters on oiled griddle or nonstick frying pan.

Note: Frozen chopped broccoli works well in this recipe.

Buckwheat (Kasha) Walnut Fritters (vegetarian with eggs)

#H 296

Yield: 40–50 pieces

1 cup	0.23 l	walnuts, chopped
2 cups	0.46 l	cooked kasha recipe #R 115, page 48
½ cup	0.11 l	flour
3	3	eggs
¼ cup	0.06 l	milk
1 tbsp	1 tbsp	salt
		oil

Toast walnuts slightly to improve flavor. Combine above ingredients to batter consistency. Fry dollar-size pancakes on griddle or in nonstick pan.

Cauliflower Fritters

#H 297

Yield: 50

2 tbsp	2 tbsp	onions, chopped
1 tbsp	1 tbsp	oil
3 cups	0.70 l	cauliflower, cooked and chopped
½ cup	0.11 l	flour
2	2	eggs
½ cup	0.11 l	light cream
¼ tsp	¼ tsp	cumin
¼ tsp	¼ tsp	nutmeg
		salt and pepper to taste
		oil

Saute onions in 1 tbsp oil until limp. Add cauliflower and toss well, remove from heat. Sprinkle with flour and blend. Mix eggs and cream, add to cauliflower mixture. Add remaining ingredients and mix well. Drop small fritters on oiled griddle or nonstick frying pan.

#H 298   ## Celeriac Fritters (vegetarian)

Yield: 50 pieces

1	1	lemon, peel and juice
3 cups	0.70 l	celeriac, very fine julienne or shredded on mandolin
3	3	eggs
½ cup	0.11 l	cake flour
½ cup	0.11 l	milk
½ cup	0.11 l	Italian parsley, coarsely chopped
1 tsp	1 tsp	coarse black pepper
		salt to taste
		oil

Grate lemon peel and reserve. Cover celeriac strips with water, add juice from lemon, bring to boil, drain. Spread out to cool. Combine remaining ingredients with grated lemon peel, add drained celeriac, blend. With tablespoon drop small fritters on oiled griddle or nonstick pan, flatten slightly, cook on both sides.

Note: The celery flavor is prominent and the fritter does not need any dip or sauce. Some customers might prefer less celery flavor; in that case 1 cup (0.23 l) celery can be substituted with same amount of zucchini julienne, which should not be boiled. It is important that the julienne is very fine and the strips are not too long.

#H 299   ## Cheese Fritters with Arugula (vegetarian)

Yield: 50 pieces

2 cups	0.46 l	arugula, chopped
16 oz	450 g	Swiss cheese, grated
8 oz	225 g	Parmesan cheese, grated
4	4	eggs
1 cup	0.23 l	flour
		oil

Wash arugula and boil 15 minutes. Chill and drain. Chop coarsely. Combine all ingredients. With teaspoon drop small fritters on oiled griddle or nonstick pan and fry on both sides.

Chestnut and Sausage Fritters

Yield: 60–75 pieces

16 oz	450 g	hot Italian sausage or sausage meat
3 cups	0.70 l	chestnuts, cooked
½ tsp	½ tsp	ginger, chopped
½ tsp	½ tsp	anise seeds, chopped
2	2	eggs
3 tbsp	3 tbsp	flour
		oil

Remove sausage from casing if applicable. Put meat in heavy skillet and brown over low heat, stirring frequently to break up meat. Drain off fat, add ginger and anise. Cool. Chop or crumble chestnuts and add to meat. Cool mixture. Combine with eggs and flour. Drop small fritters in hot oil.

Note: Canned chestnuts, *not sweet,* can be used. Dried chestnuts are cheaper and require soaking overnight and boiling. Fresh chestnuts must be split and baked in the oven, fried in the fryer, or microwaved. The yield on fresh chestnuts varies depending on the moisture content and freshness of the nuts.

#H 301

Chicken and Cabbage Galette

Yield: 100 pieces

40 oz	*1.12 kg*	*green cabbage*
1 cup	*0.23 l*	*scallions, diced*
		salt and pepper
		poultry mousse recipe #R 140, page 60
2 cups	*0.46 l*	*fresh bread crumbs*
2 cups	*0.46 l*	*oil*

Coarsely chop cabbage and scallions, add 1 cup (0.23 l) water. Put in casserole, bring to boil, cover and braise 30 minutes. All liquid should be evaporated; drain if necessary. Chop cabbage coarsely in food processor, the resulting cabbage should be about 2 cups (0.46 l). Heat ¼ cup (0.06 l) oil in pan and saute cabbage until dry and almost brown. Chill. Season. Blend chilled cabbage with poultry mousse. Shape small patties, about 1½ in. (37 mm) across and ¼ in. (7 mm) high, pat with bread crumbs. Panfry with remaining oil on both sides until brown and cooked.

Note: The product is shaped easiest with a small ice cream scoop. The mixture can also be spread on an oiled sheet pan, covered with foil, and baked at 450°F/230°C. When cooled, it can be cut into bite-size squares or triangles.

Chicken and vegetable galette recipe #H 302, this page.

Chicken and Vegetable Galette

#H 302

Yield: 100 pieces

2 cups	0.46 l	assorted vegetables, cooked and coarsely chopped
½ cup	0.11 l	scallions, diced
		salt and pepper
		poultry mousse recipe #R 140, page 60
2 cups	0.46 l	fresh bread crumbs
2 cups	0.46 l	oil

Combine cold, drained vegetables with scallions and poultry mousse. Shape small patties, about 1½ in. (37 mm) across and ¼ in. (7 mm) high, pat with bread crumbs. Panfry on both sides until brown and cooked.

French toast with calf's liver and sage recipe #H 303, this page.

#H 303   French Toast with Calf's Liver and Sage

Yield: 48

24	24	extra-thin sandwich bread (Peppridge Farm), slices
24 oz	670 g	calf's liver, in one piece
8 oz	225 g	butter
4 tbsp	4 tbsp	fresh sage, chopped
		salt and pepper
6	6	eggs
1½ cups	0.34 l	light cream
		oil for frying

Remove skin from calf's liver and place in freezer until almost frozen. On meat slicer cut thin pieces about ¼ in. (7 mm) thick. Separate slices and return to freezer. Soften butter and spread evenly on 12 bread slices. Sprinkle with sage. Place frozen liver slices on top, sprinkle generously with salt and pepper and cover with second slice. Wrap and return to freezer. Combine eggs and cream. Dip slices in mixture while still frozen, fry on griddle until brown on both sides. Place in oven if needed to cook the liver center to a lovely pink.

Note: It is important to keep the slices frozen to prevent blood staining the bread. The liver should still be medium rare. Make sure servers know what they are serving. Some people do not like liver, although chicken liver and bacon used to be a popular hors d'oeuvre.

French Toast with Smoked Salmon   **#H 304**

Yield: 100

50	50	extra thin sandwich bread (Peppridge Farm), slices
		butter, soft
100 slices	100 slices	smoked salmon
2 tbsp	2 tbsp	dill, chopped
6	6	eggs
1½ cups	0.34 l	light cream
		oil for frying

Lay 25 slices bread on table, lightly spread with butter, and put 4 slices salmon on each bread slice. Sprinkle with dill. Lightly spread second slice with butter and place on top of sandwiches. Press down, wrap, and refrigerate/freeze. Trim crust and cut each sandwich in 4 pieces. Combine eggs and cream. Dip slices in mixture and fry on griddle until brown on both sides.

Note: It is important to use very thin bread, because the egg mixture will not penetrate thick bread slices easily. Sandwiches can be fried before being cut.

#H 305

Garbanzo Fritters (vegetarian)

Yield: 120 pieces

1 #10 can	*1 #10 can*	*chickpeas, cooked*
1 tbsp	*1 tbsp*	*oil*
½ tbsp	*½ tbsp*	*garlic, chopped*
½ cup	*0.11 l*	*tahini paste*
½ cup	*0.11 l*	*sesame seeds*
¼ cup	*0.06 l*	*mint, chopped*
¼ tsp	*¼ tsp*	*cardamom*
¼ tsp	*¼ tsp*	*ground hot pepper*
1 tbsp	*1 tbsp*	*salt*
2	*2*	*eggs*
4 tbsp	*4 tbsp*	*flour*
		oil

Drain chickpeas, discard water. There should be about 72 oz (2 kg) of the drained product. Chop coarsely in food processor. Add remaining ingredients except oil. Drop little fritters on hot griddle or into nonstick frying pan.

#H 306

Ham and Sauerkraut Fritters

Yield: 50 pieces

2 cups	*0.46 l*	*sauerkraut, drained*
2 cups	*0.46 l*	*ham, diced small*
½ tbsp	*½ tbsp*	*caraway seeds, chopped*
2	*2*	*eggs*
4 tbsp	*4 tbsp*	*flour*
		oil

Chop sauerkraut coarsely in food processor, add all other ingredients. Mix, but do not puree. Form small fritters with tablespoon and fry on griddle or in nonstick frying pan.

Mixed Vegetable Fritters (vegetarian)

#H 307

mixed frozen or fresh vegetables
eggs
flour
oil
salt and pepper

Any kind of mixed vegetables will work. If fresh vegetables are used, it is advisable to blanch (precook) them, chill, and drain. The amount of eggs and flour varies according to the moisture content of the vegetables. The type of flour used can also vary and can range from buckwheat to whole wheat. It is advisable to make a sample fritter to make sure the fritter does not fall apart or is too solid.

Parmesan Cheese Fritters (vegetarian)

#H 308

Yield: 50 pieces

1½ cups	0.34 l	Parmesan cheese, grated
3 cups	0.70 l	white, fresh bread crumbs
4 oz	112 g	butter, melted
5	5	eggs
3 tbsp	3 tbsp	parsley, chopped
¼ tsp	¼ tsp	nutmeg

Combine above ingredients. Batter will get stiffer as it rests. Shape little balls and fry on griddle or nonstick frying pan until golden brown.

#H 309

Polenta and Bacalao Cakes (vegetarian)

Yield: 100

24 oz	670 g	*salted codfish*
		water and/or milk
1¼ cup	0.29 l	*coarse cornmeal (polenta)*
¼ cup	0.06 l	*parsley, chopped*
2	2	*eggs*
½ cup	0.11 l	*red pimento, diced very fine*
		oil

Soak bacalao overnight in cold water. Discard water, cover with half water and half milk, bring to boil. Simmer ½ hour or until fish is flaky. Drain fish off and save 32 oz (0.92 l) stock. Pick fish over to remove all bones, flake. Bring fish stock to boil, stir in polenta, cover and cook over low flame 30 minutes. Remove from heat. Add flaked fish, parsley, eggs, and diced pimento. Shape into small cakes, about 1 in. (25 mm) across. Cook on griddle or on nonstick frying pan.

Note: Taste stock; if too salty dilute with water. To shape cakes the mixture can be spread about ½ in. (12 mm) high on oiled sheet pan, covered with foil and refrigerated overnight. Next day the cakes can be cut with a cookie cutter. The mixture can also be shaped with slightly oiled hands or with an ice cream scoop # 24.

#H 310

Polenta Fritters with Dried Porcini Mushrooms (vegetarian)

Yield: 50 pieces

5 oz	140 g	*porcini mushrooms, dried polenta recipe #R 121, page 51, adjusted without cheese*
1 tbsp	1 tbsp	*salt*
¼ cup	0.06 l	*Italian parsley, chopped*
		oil

Wash mushrooms to remove any sand and soak overnight. Bring to boil and boil about 1 hour, cool. Lift mushrooms from stock and chop coarsely. Save stock. Make polenta according to recipe but substitute some liquid with mushroom stock. Season with salt. Add chopped mushrooms and parsley to polenta, mix well. Spread on oiled baking sheet ¾ in. (18 mm) thick, cover and cool. Cut into suitable bite-size pieces and griddle fry.

Potato Blue Cheese Cakes (vegetarian)

#H 311

Yield: 75 pieces

64 oz	1.80 kg	Russet potatoes (about 8)
8 oz	225 g	blue cheese
1 cup	0.23 l	flour
1 tsp	1 tsp	nutmeg
1	1	egg
		oil

Bake potatoes, peel and put through ricer while still hot. Let mixture cool. Puree blue cheese in food processor. On pastry board combine potatoes, cheese, flour, nutmeg, and egg to make stiff dough. Shape little patties and cook on slightly oiled griddle.

Note: The amount of flour needed depends on the moisture content of the potatoes and of the cheese. Make a sample and add more flour if patties do not stay together.

Potato Latkes (Fritters) (vegetarian)

#H 312

Yield: 100–120 pieces

20	20	baking potatoes, 80 size
2	2	parsley, bunches
8	8	onions, medium size
6 cups	1.40 l	matzo meal
14	14	eggs
		salt and pepper
		oil for frying

Peel potatoes. Grind potatoes, parsley, and onions in meat grinder with medium plate. Put in colander to drain for about 1 hour. Discard water. Mix potatoes with remaining ingredients. With spoon drop little fritters in hot oil and panfry on both sides.

Note: Latkes can be served with applesauce. If served without sauce or dip, the mixture can be flavored with spices or herbs.

Quail Egg Silver Dollars

Yield: 50 pieces

50	50	*brioche slices, ¼ in. (7 mm) thick and 2 in. (50 mm) across*
½ cup	0.11 l	*melted butter*
½ cup	0.11 l	*Parmesan cheese, grated*
50	50	*quail eggs*
		oil

Brush rounds with butter, sprinkle with cheese and bake in oven until brown and crisp. Carefully fry quail eggs sunny-side up on griddle. Cut away excessive egg whites with same cutter as has been used for the brioche slices. Place eggs and brioche rounds.

Note: The item can be varied by spreading the brioche with pesto, sun-dried tomato pesto or other suitable spreads. Chives and/or other herbs can be added to the butter spread. Smoked salmon or thin slices of ham can be put on the brioche. The item looks pretty but is awkward to eat in one bite. Plates should be available. It lends itself to breakfast receptions. Use left-over brioche for crumbs.

Red Lentil Fritters

Yield: 50 pieces

8 oz	225 g	*Italian sausage*
½ cup	0.11 l	*onions, chopped*
2 tbsp	2 tbsp	*curry powder*
12 oz	335 g	*red lentils*
½ cup	0.11 l	*red pepper, parcooked and diced*
2	2	*eggs*
4 tbsp	4 tbsp	*flour*
		salt
		oil

Squeeze meat out of sausage casing. Put sausage meat in heavy sauce pot and saute slowly, stirring frequently to break meat into small pieces. When meat is cooked, drain off fat, add onions and cook over slow heat until onions are soft. Add curry powder, lentils, and cover with 6 cups (1.40 l) water. Boil until lentils are soft and mushy. About all water should evaporate. The cooking process will take about 1 hour. During the last phase frequent stirring is necessary and additional water might have to be added if too much has evaporated before lentils are soft. Season to taste and cool. Add red pepper, eggs, and flour. If mixture is too liquid, add fresh white bread crumbs to thicken. Drop fritters on oiled griddle or into nonstick frying pan.

Note: It is always advisable to make a sample fritter to make sure it will hold together.

Rösti Potatoes   #H 315

Yield: 50 pieces

4 cups	0.92 l	cooked potatoes, shredded
4 tbsp	4 tbsp	chives, chopped
		salt and pepper
		oil

The potatoes should be Russet type and cooked in the jacket. Peel when cold and shred on grater into long shreds. Season with chives, salt, and pepper. Heat oil in small nonstick pans and place a layer of potatoes about ½ in. (12 mm) thick. Pat down with spatula. Cook until brown, flip over and cook again until brown and crisp. The potato cakes should be very crisp and dry. Cut into small wedges and serve warm with salsa or other dips.

Note: Make sure the Rösti potatoes are not fatty; drain on paper towel if necessary. The item is served best with plates.

#H 316   ## Savoy Cabbage and Bacon Fritters

Yield: 25–30 pieces

16 oz	450 g	savoy cabbage
4 oz	112 g	bacon, ground or cut in very small dice
½ cup	0.11 l	onions, chopped
1 tsp	1 tsp	caraway seeds, chopped
1 tsp	1 tsp	salt
½ tsp	½ tsp	butcher ground pepper
2	2	eggs
2 tbsp	2 tbsp	flour
		oil

Coarsely chop savoy cabbage, wash well and drain. Render bacon until crisp, drain excessive fat. Add onions, saute until onions are limp, add remaining ingredients and 1 cup (0.23 l) water, cover, and braise 30 minutes over low heat. Occasionally a little water must be added. The mixture should be cooked, and almost all moisture should have evaporated. Remove from heat, cool, drain if necessary, chop coarsely in food processor. Add eggs and flour. Mix well. Drop fritter on oiled griddle or fry in nonstick frying pan.

Note: It is always advisable to make a sample fritter to make sure it will stick together.

#H 317   ## Semolina Mushroom Cakes

Yield: 100

20 oz	560 g	mushrooms
¼ cup	0.06 l	sherry wine
2 cups	0.46 l	light cream
1 cup	0.23 l	semolina
		salt and pepper to taste
½ cup	0.11 l	red pepper, diced very small
2 tbsp	2 tbsp	parsley, chopped
2	2	eggs
		oil

Wash mushrooms; make sure all sand is removed. Chop coarsely in food processor. Put mushrooms in heavy pot, add wine, cover, and bring to boil. When mixture is boiling add cream and semolina, stir, bring to boil, cover and simmer 20 minutes. Blanch pepper. Add pepper and parsley and eggs to semolina mixture. Spread an oiled baking sheet about ¾ in. (19 mm) thick, cover and refrigerate. Cut into bite-size lozenges or circles. Brush with oil and cook on griddle or nonstick frying pan.

Note: Cream of wheat can be substituted. The exact amount of semolina needed is hard to estimate because it depends on the moisture content of the mushrooms. If mixture is too soft, thicken with fresh bread crumbs.

Spaghetti Squash and Ginger Fritters (vegetarian)   #H 318

Yield: 30–40 pieces

48 oz	675 g	*spaghetti squash*
¼ tsp	¼ tsp	*jalapeño pepper, chopped*
1 tsp	1 tsp	*ginger, chopped*
1 tsp	1 tsp	*turmeric*
2	2	*eggs*
4 tbsp	4 tbsp	*flour*
		oil

Split squash, remove seeds, brush with oil, cover with foil, and bake about 1 hour at 375°/190°C. Cool. Scrape out pulp with spoon, chop coarsely if necessary. Combine with all ingredients. Drop small fritter on griddle or into nonstick frying pan.

Note: It is always advisable to make a sample fritter to make sure it will hold together.

#H 319

Spinach and Parmesan Cheese Fritters

Yield: 50 pieces

4 tbsp	4 tbsp	onions, chopped
1 tsp	1 tsp	garlic, chopped
4 tbsp	4 tbsp	olive oil
1 tsp	1 tsp	black pepper, ground
½ tsp	½ tsp	nutmeg, ground
4 cups	0.92 l	frozen spinach or fresh spinach, cooked and chopped
½ tbsp	½ tbsp	salt
4	4	eggs
1 cup	0.23 l	flour
2 cups	0.46 l	Parmesan cheese, grated

Saute onions and garlic in oil, cool. Add remaining ingredients. Drop small fritters on griddle or fry in nonstick frying pan.

Note: It is always advisable to make a sample fritter to make sure it will stick together.

#H 320

Spinach, Watercress, and Water Chestnut Fritters

Yield: 50 pieces

2 bunches	2 bunches	watercress
4 tbsp	4 tbsp	onions, chopped
1 tsp	1 tsp	garlic, chopped
3 tbsp	3 tbsp	olive oil
1 tsp	1 tsp	black pepper, ground
4 tbsp	4 tbsp	soy sauce or tamari sauce
1 tbsp		sesame oil
2 cups	0.46 l	frozen spinach or fresh spinach, cooked and chopped
2 cups	0.46 l	water chestnuts, canned, chopped
4	4	eggs
1 cup	0.23 l	flour

Cut watercress across stems into ¼ in. (7 mm) pieces, wash well to remove all sand. Boil (or steam) about 10 minutes, chill, and drain. Saute onions and garlic in olive oil, cool. Combine all ingredients in food processor to make coarse batter. Drop fritters on griddle or into nonstick frying pan.

Note: It is always advisable to make a sample fritter to make sure it will hold together.

Spinach, Watercress, and Swiss Cheese Fritters   **#H 321**

Yield: 50 pieces

> use ingredients of recipe #H 318, on page 241, but substitute
>   Parmesan cheese with Swiss cheese

Follow instructions in recipe #H 318.

Note: It is always advisable to make a sample fritter to make sure it will hold together.

Wild Rice, Smoked Salmon, and Chives Fritters   **#H 322**

Yield: 40 pieces

2 cups	0.46 l	cooked wild rice recipe #R 127, page 53
½ cup	0.11 l	flour
2	2	eggs
¼ cup	0.06 l	milk
3 tbsp	3 tbsp	chives, diced
10 oz	280 g	smoked salmon
		oil

Make batter with above ingredients except smoked salmon. Cut salmon in fine julienne. Drop small batches of batter on griddle or into nonstick frying pan. Sprinkle smoked salmon on top before batter solidifies. Turn over and cook on both sides.

Note: Items can be served with horseradish mixed with sour cream. It is always advisable to make a sample fritter to make sure it will hold together.

#H 323   # Wild Rice and Sausage Fritters

Yield: 40 pieces

½ cup	0.11 l	seedless raisins
8 oz	225 g	coarse pork sausage meat
2 cups	0.46 l	cooked wild rice recipe #R 127, page 53
½ cup	0.11 l	flour
3	3	eggs
1 tbsp	1 tbsp	cumin
1 tbsp	1 tbsp	anise seeds, ground
1 tbsp	1 tbsp	salt
		oil

Soak raisins in cold water. Saute sausage meat until cooked and brown, break into small pieces frequently. The mixture should be crumbly. Drain off fat, cool. Drain raisins. Combine all ingredients. Drop fritters on griddle or into nonstick frying pan.

Note: It is always advisable to make a sample fritter to make sure it will hold together.

Roasted Items

#H 324   # Roasted Brussels Sprouts

Yield: 50 pieces

50	50	fresh brussels sprouts, large
1 tsp	1 tsp	savory, dried
1 tsp	1 tsp	thyme, dried
		salt to taste
1 cup	0.23 l	olive oil
		sprigs of fresh thyme

Clean vegetable if necessary. Combine brussels sprouts with dried herbs, cover with water, salt to taste and boil 5 minutes. Drain. Roast brussels sprouts with oil and thyme sprigs until lightly brown.

Note: Item should be served with toothpicks. Roasted thyme can be served also and makes a nice garnish.

Duckling Breast with Sour Cherries

Yield: 100 pieces

2 each	2 each	Barberie drake duckling double breast, about 30–35 oz (840–980 g)
		oil
2 cups	0.46 l	sour cherries, frozen
1 tsp	1 tsp	cayenne pepper
2 cups	0.46 l	poultry mousse recipe #R 140, page 60
1 cup	0.23 l	sh bread crumbs

Remove skin from duckling breasts. (Skin can be used in recipe #H 198 tartlets with smoked duckling). Oil breast and quickly grill on both side to stiffen meat, but do not cook through. Cool. In food processor coarsely chop cherries and add all other ingredients. Slice duckling meat into slices and lay out on table. Fill with cherry/poultry filling (use pastry bag). Roll up and secure with toothpick. Brush with oil and broil until filling is cooked.

Note: Frozen sour cherries are often mixed with 20 percent sugar. If this is the case they should be rinsed quickly with cold water. Some residual sugar is acceptable and will enhance the flavor of the dish. If sour cherries without sugar are used, 1 tbsp sugar should be added to the dish.

#H 326

Lamb Chop Marinated with Mint

For marinade:

Yield, marinade: 50

1 cup	0.23 l	red wine vinegar
1 cup	0.23 l	balsamic vinegar
½ cup	0.11 l	oil
½ cup	0.11 l	mint leaves, chopped
2 tbsp	2 tbsp	butcher ground pepper
1 tbsp	1 tbsp	lemon peel, grated
½ tsp	½ tsp	garlic, chopped
		salt to taste

For lamb:

The lamb chops should be completely fat free and small. The bones should be scraped to be free of fat. If domestic lamb is used buy Hotel-Size, Eight Rib Rack, MBG # 204 in the smallest available weight range, which is about 3 to 5 lb (1.35 to 2.25 kg). Each rack yields 16 chops. New Zealand lamb is smaller and a single rack, boned except the rib bones, weighs 6 to 7 oz (176 to 200 g). Each rack yields 6 to 7 small chops.

Combine marinade ingredients. Marinate chops for 24 hours. Grill or broil chops as needed. They should be medium.

Note: The bones can be wrapped in foil to prevent burning or discoloration. Provision must be made to collect the bones. A second server with a deep platter should follow the first server for this purpose.

Lemongrass Sausage

Yield: 50 pieces

32 oz	900 g	pork shoulder, cut in 1 in. (25 mm) cubes
16 oz	450 g	fresh pork fat back, cut in 1 in. (25 mm) cubes
½ tbsp	½ tbsp	salt
1 tsp	1 tsp	sugar
¼ tsp	¼ tsp	butcher ground pepper
1 tbsp	1 tbsp	Hungarian paprika
½ tsp	½ tsp	garlic, rubbed with salt to fine paste
½ tbsp	½ tbsp	lemongrass, dried and ground (or 1 tbsp chopped fresh)
6 each	6 each	lemons, grated peel
1 oz	0.03 l	pepper vodka
		sausage casings, natural

Marinate pork and fat back with seasonings overnight. Grind meat through medium coarse plate of meat grinder. Fill casings with mixture and tie off small sausages about 1½ in. (37 mm) long. Before use, cover with water and bring to boil, drain and chill. Roast sausages as needed until brown. Serve with mustard or with #R 167 green mint puree or #R 168 green lime dip, page 73.

Note: Sausage casings should be about ½ in. (12 mm) in diameter. They must be washed well to remove salt and occasionally soaked overnight in cold water. Sausage stuffing funnel attachment is needed to stuff sausages.

#H 327 ## Mint Sausage

Yield: 50–60 pieces

32 oz	900 g	lamb shoulder, not too much fat, cut in 1 in. (25 mm) cubes
16 oz	450 g	fresh pork fat back, cut in 1 in. (25 mm) cubes
½ tbsp	½ tbsp	salt
1 tsp	1 tsp	butcher ground pepper
½ tsp	½ tsp	garlic, rubbed with salt to fine paste
3 tbsp	3 tbsp	fresh mint, chopped
2 oz	56 g	white crème de menthe liquor
1 each	1 each	navel orange, grated peel
1 cup	0.23 l	pine nuts, chopped
		natural sausage casings

Marinate lamb and pork fat back with seasonings overnight. Grind meat through medium coarse plate of meat grinder. Fill casings with mixture and tie off small sausages about 1½ in. (37 mm) long. Before use, cover with water and bring to boil, drain and chill. Roast sausages as needed until brown. Serve with mustard or with #R 167 green mint puree or #R 168 green lime dip, page 73.

Note: Sausage casings should be about ½ in. (12 mm) in diameter. They must be washed well to remove salt and occasionally soaked overnight in cold water. Sausage stuffing funnel attachment is needed to stuff sausages.

Quail Breast with Rosemary

#H 328

Yield: 50 pieces

25	25	whole quails (5–6 oz/140–170 g each)
		fresh rosemary
8 oz	225 g	poultry (turkey or chicken) meat, ground
½ cup	0.11 l	heavy cream
1	1	egg white
2 tbsp	2 tbsp	parsley, chopped
½ cup	0.11 l	pistachio nuts, peeled
		salt and pepper
		rice wafer paper
		oil

Bone quails. Remove breasts and skin. Marinate breasts with oil and rosemary overnight. Bone legs and add leg meat to poultry meat. Process in food processor with cream, egg white, salt, pepper, and some rosemary to smooth stuffing. Add pistachio nuts. Drain marinated quail breasts and pat dry. With pastry bag put a little stuffing on inside of each breast piece. Wrap in rice wafer paper according to instructions on page 37. Brush with oil and broil or roast 10 minutes or until stuffing is cooked.

Note: The item is labor-intensive because boning the birds can be laborious. Boneless quail breasts are available and can be used in the recipe above, except that the stuffing would not contain any quail meat. In this case, the poultry meat should be increased to 12 oz (340 g).

#H 330

Pork Tenderloin Silver Dollars

Yield: 50 pieces

5	5	pork tenderloin
½ cup	0.11 l	sweet sherry wine
		sage, fresh
		salt to taste
		cream cheese dough recipe #HT 101, page 29
2 tbsp	2 tbsp	oil
½ cup	0.11 l	prepared mustard, sharp

Trim pork tenderloins, cut of tapered end. The muscle should look like a tube. Marinate in sherry wine and sage stems overnight. Roll dough about ¼ in. (7 mm) thick, cut 1½ in. (37 mm) circles and bake at 400°F/200°C. Drain pork loins, salt to taste, brush with oil, and roast until cooked but not dry. Keep warm. As needed, pipe small amount of mustard on each dough circle, place slice of pork on top and decorate with sage leaf.

#H 331

Roast Salted Whole Shrimp

Yield: 100 pieces

100	100	small shrimp, in shell, head on, 50 count
		oil
		coarse (kosher) salt

Stir-fry shrimp quickly in very hot pan until very crisp. They should not be watery. Sprinkle with coarse salt.

Note: Shrimp must be cooked in small amounts so they will stay crisp. They can be eaten with shell and head on.

Roast Beef Tenderloin

#H 332

Yield: 50–60 pieces

1 each	*1 each*	*beef tenderloin, MBG # 189a or 190, about 5 lb (2.25 kg)*
		salt and pepper
		oil
50–60	*50–60*	*baguette bread, slices*
		butcher ground pepper
		mustard
		fresh thyme, optional

Cut off head and tail of tenderloin. It should now weigh about 4 lb (1.8 kg). Use head and tail for other dishes. Rub with salt and pepper, oil and roast at high heat about 25 minutes. Let rest at least 20 minutes on warm place to let juices circulate. Toast baguette slices on one side only. For service, slice meat in half and cut into ¼ in. (7 mm) pieces. Place on toasted side of baguette, sprinkle with coarse (butcher ground) pepper. Put a dab of mustard on top. Garnish with a small thyme snippet if desired.

Note: This item is sometimes not served efficiently. The bread should be about ¼ in. (7 mm) thick. If toasted on one side only it is normally not so dry that it will crumble easily when eaten. Often sauces are served with the meat, which can make the dish messy.

Spoon items

Spoon hors d'oeuvres have come into fashion, although they are not very practical. A small amount of food is placed on dessert spoons and the spoons are placed on a platter. One server circulates with the platter, closely followed by a second server with an empty platter for the soiled spoons. The spoons should be warm, but not too hot to touch, and the food cools quickly. All ingredients must be cut small enough to be swallowed in one bite.

#H 333 ## Beef Chili

Yield: 50 servings

32 oz	900 g	chuck, ground
1 cup	0.23 l	onions, chopped
1 tsp	1 tsp	garlic, chopped
4 tbsp	4 tbsp	chili powder
½ cup	0.11 l	tomato puree
1 cup	0.23 l	kidney beans, cooked
½ cup	0.11 l	green peppers, chopped
		Jalapeño peppers to taste
		salt to taste

Roast ground meat in heavy-bottom pot, stir frequently to break up pieces. Drain off most fat. Add onions, garlic, and chili powder, saute slowly. Add remaining ingredients, except beans, and cook for about 1 hour. Add beans, bring to boil, season to taste. If mixture is too thin, thicken with cornstarch.

Note: Jalapeño pepper is very hot and should be used with caution.

Hungarian Rice and Pork #H 334

Yield: 50 servings

8 oz	225 g	pork tenderloin, cut into very small dice
¼ cup	0.06 l	oil
½ cup	0.11 l	onions, chopped
1 tbsp	1 tbsp	Hungarian paprika
¼ tsp	¼ tsp	marjoram, chopped
¼ tsp	¼ tsp	caraway seeds, chopped
¼ tsp	¼ tsp	garlic, chopped
2 cups	0.46 l	rice
4 cups	0.92 l	chicken stock
		salt to taste
½ cup	0.11 l	sour cream
4 oz	112 g	cheese, grated

Saute pork in oil until brown, add onions and spices. Saute 5 minutes. Add rice and stock. Bring to boil, cover and simmer 25 minutes. Add cheese and sour cream.

Risotto with Dried Porcini (Cèpes) #H 335

Yield: 50 servings

4 oz	112 g	porcini (mushrooms), dried
		risotto recipe #R 160, page 69

Soak porcini mushrooms overnight. Lift out of water and check for sand at the bottom. Slowly pour soaking water back over porcini, but leave sand at the bottom behind. Boil dried mushrooms until soft, or about 1 hour. Add more water if needed. Drain and save stock. Chop mushrooms coarsely. Use stock, supplemented with chicken stock when making risotto. Add chopped mushrooms toward the end of the cooking process.

Note: Risotto should be almost runny, but the rice kernels should be solid to the bite in the center. It will thicken when standing, and should be diluted with chicken stock as needed. Obviously it should not be so runny that is runs off the spoons.

#H 337

Saffron Risotto with Salami

Yield: 50 servings

¼ tsp	¼ tsp	*saffron*
8 oz	112 g	*salami, cut into very small dice*
		risotto recipe #R 160, page 69

Soak saffron in one cup chicken broth for one hour, bring to boil and steep. Do not drain. Make risotto as described in recipe, add saffron stock when cooking the rice. Add salami when adding cheese and butter.

Note: Risotto should be almost runny, but the rice kernels should be solid to the bite in the center. It will thicken when standing, and should be diluted with chicken stock as needed. Obviously it should not be so runny that is runs off the spoons.

#H 338

Sherry Mushrooms

Yield: 50 servings

mushrooms with sherry, recipe #R 156, page 67

Fill spoons as needed. Make sure mushroom mixture is not too thin. If necessary, thicken with a little cornstarch.

Steamed Items

Steamed food is gaining in popularity because it is often low in fat. Small vegetables can be cut into bite-size pieces or served whole and served with a dipping sauce. They can also be stuffed, steamed, or baked.

Other steamed items include stuffing wrapped in precooked vegetable leaves or in rice wafer paper. In some cases, the stuffing can be rolled first in cooked leaves and than in rice wafer paper. Many stuffings often contain fat to make them soft and palatable.

Food wrapped in rice wafer paper will stick to the steamer basket if the basket and the food itself are not oiled. After the food is steamed it should rest a few minutes before it is served. Instructions on how to work with rice wafer paper are on page 37 in Chapter 4.

Oriental cooking has many steamed dumplings. See the international hors d'oeuvres section on page 210 for ideas.

Steamed Baby Vegetables with Dipping Sauces   **#H 339**

baby vegetables or young vegetables cut in bite-size chunks
(the selection should be colorful)

Wash vegetables and steam until hot and crisp. The length of cooking time depends on the size and maturity of the vegetable. The vegetables should be firm when served. Some will require toothpicks.

Note: Suitable dipping sauces are: asparagus dip recipe #R 166, page 72; green lime dip recipe #R 168, page 73; lemon chutney recipe #R 169, page 74; roast corn relish recipe #R 172, page 75; roasted tomato salsa recipe #R 173, page 76; salsa recipe #R 174, page 76; taramasalata dip recipe #R 175, page 77; and tomatillo dip recipe #R 176, page 77.

#H 340

Filled Steamed Baby Vegetables

Many baby vegetables can be filled. The easiest to handle are pattypan squash and tiny turnips.

vegetables of choice
fish mousse, poultry mousse, miso, or other filling of choice
oil

Cut top or bottom of vegetable and keep as lid. Scoop out vegetable. Coarsely chop vegetables that have been scooped out and steam for 5 minutes. Chill. Mix vegetables with filling, adjust seasoning. Fill cavity generously (use pastry bag), place lid on top. Put vegetables in shallow baking pan, brush with oil, cover with foil, and steam until filling is cooked.

Steamed pattypan squash recipe #H 340, this page, filled with poultry mousse and miso.

Steamed Chili with Corn Masa

#H 341

Yield: 50 pieces

¼ cup	0.06 l	lard
1¼ cup	0.29 l	warm water
2 cups	0.46 l	masa harina
½ tsp	½ tsp	salt
½ tsp	½ tsp	cumin powder
50	50	mild poblano chili, canned, peeled
		oil
		rice wafer paper

Combine lard and water until lard is melted. Add masa and spices to make stiff dough. Let rest one hour. Wrap masa and chili in rice wafer paper according to directions on page 37. Oil and steam 20 minutes.

Note: The sharpness of chili varies greatly. The seeds and veins are sharper than the flesh. Green poblano chili is probably the mildest and is available canned.

Steamed Grave Lax in Spinach Leaves

#H 342

Yield: 50 pieces

40 oz	1.12 kg	grave lax according to recipe #R 178, page 78
50	50	spinach leaves, large and flat
		egg whites

Remove skin from salmon and cut into 50 equal size cubes. Quickly blanch spinach leaves, chill in cold water. Carefully remove leaves and lay on kitchen table. Brush leaves with egg whites mixed with equal amount of cold water. Wrap salmon to make neat bundles. Steam 5 minutes, serve warm.

Note: The egg white acts as glue to keep the bundles together.

#H 343

Steamed Lettuce Leaves Filled with Fish Mousse

Yield: 50 pieces

25	25	*Boston lettuce leaves*
		rice wafer paper
		fish mousse recipe #R
		136, page 58

Carefully separate leaves and wash. Boil in plenty of water for 3 minutes. Chill under cold running water, add ice to hasten chilling if necessary. Carefully remove leaves from water, one by one. Cut rice wafer paper into 4 x 4 in. (100 x 100 mm) pieces, place lettuce leaves (cut) into suitable size on top, place fish mousse on top. Shape into bundle with twisted rice wafer paper on top. Place on oiled sheet pans, chill or freeze. Oil steamer basket and steam 10 minutes over gentle heat.

#H 344

Steamed Lettuce Leaves Filled with Sushi Rice

Yield: 50 pieces

25	25	*green leaves of Boston let-*
		tuce, outsides
		sushi rice recipe #R 126,
		page 53

Cook leaves in rapidly boiling water, chill in ice water. Carefully remove leaves and place on sheet pan. Shape rice with wet hands into 50 little balls, chill. Spread out leaves, remove center spine, cut into even pieces about 3 x 2 in. (75 x 50 mm). Roll rice in leaves, place seam side down in oiled steamer basket. Steam until hot.

Steamed Spinach Leaves Filled with Poultry Mousse

#H 345

Yield: 50 pieces

50	50	*spinach leaves, flat and large*
		poultry mousse recipe #R 140, page 60
		rice wafer paper

Follow instructions detailed in recipe #H 343 but replace fish mousse with poultry mousse, and lettuce with spinach.

Three varieties of food wrapped in rice wafer paper ready to be steamed.

#H 346

Steamed Shrimp with Corn Masa

Yield: 50 pieces

¼ cup	0.06 l	lard
1¼ cup	0.29 l	warm water
2 cups	0.46 l	masa harina
½ tsp	½ tsp	salt
½ tsp	½ tsp	cumin powder
50	50	shrimp, 22/24 size, cooked and peeled
50	50	green pepper, pieces
25	25	rice wafer paper, sheets

Make masa dough according to direction in recipe #H 341, page 257. Split shrimp. Quickly boil peppers for 1 minute, chill and drain. Cut rice wafer paper in half. Make bundles with rice wafer paper according to directions on page 37. Fill bundles with 2 pieces shrimp and 1 piece pepper. Chill bundles, oil and steam 15 minutes.

#H 347

Steamed Surimi Sticks and Seaweed

Yield: 100 pieces

25	25	nori (seaweed), sheets
25	25	rice wafer paper, sheets
20	20	surimi sticks
20	20	cucumbers, seedless, cut into 7 in. (180 mm) sticks
6 cups	1.40 l	sushi rice, cooked, recipe #R 126, page 53
4 tbsp	4 tbsp	sesame seeds, toasted

Cut each sheet of nori and rice wafer paper in 4 pieces. Cut surimi sticks in 5 pieces each. Cut cucumber sticks in 5 pieces each. Place rice wafer paper pieces, one at a time, on a moist surface, top with nori, surimi, cucumber, and rice. Sprinkle with sesame seeds. Make neat bundles and steam in well oiled basket about 5 minutes. Cool slightly before service.

Steamed Sweetbreads

#H 348

Yield: 50 pieces

32 oz	900 g	sweetbreads
½ tbsp	½ tbsp	salt
1	1	bay leaf
4–6	4–6	peppercorns
16 oz	450 g	poultry mousse recipe #R 140, page 60
1 cup	0.23 l	hazelnuts, chopped
¼ cup	0.06 l	parsley, chopped
2 oz	0.06 l	brandy
25	25	rice wafer paper, sheets

Soak sweetbreads in water overnight. Drain, cover with water and boil with salt, bay leaf, and peppercorns until soft. Cool in stock. Carefully separate membranes from meat. There should be about 2 cups (0.46 l) of meat broken into little pieces. Combine with poultry mousse, hazelnuts, parsley, and brandy. With ice cream scoop # 30 portion out 50 mounds on an oiled sheet pan. Do not fill scoop all the way. Freeze. Wrap in rice wafer paper according to pictures and page 37. Make little upright bundles with a twisted top. Steam in well oiled steamer basket about 5 minutes over low heat.

Note: The length of cooking time for sweetbreads varies greatly. Sweetbreads from young animals will cook in about ½ hour, from older animals it will take considerably longer. Check frequently.

Whiskey Shrimp

#H 349

Yield: 50 pieces

50	50	shrimps, 16/20 size
2	2	lemons
¼ cup	0.06 l	olive oil
1 tsp	1 tsp	fresh tarragon, chopped
½ cup	0.11 l	tomato ketchup
½ cup	0.11 l	whiskey
		cayenne pepper to taste

Peel, devein, and wash shrimp. Grate lemon peel, squeeze juice. Combine all ingredients, cover and bring to boil. Serve at once with toothpicks.

Note: Normally there is enough moisture to steam shrimp. If ketchup is very thick, a little water might have to be added to start the steaming process. When shrimp are done the sauce should cling to them.

7

INGREDIENTS, COOKING TERMS, AND EQUIPMENT

Alphabetical List of Ingredients Mentioned in This Book, or Useful for a Caterer

ACHIOTE (ANNATTO) Reddish/yellowish seeds from the tropical annatto tree. The very hard seeds are used as a dye and as a flavoring agent. Available also as paste. The color is fat soluble and the seeds must be cooked slowly in oil until the oil is yellow. The oil is used, the seeds are inedible and are discarded. Available by weight in grocery stores that sell Hispanic products.

AMCHOOR Also known as mango powder, or Amchur powder. It is made from unripe mangoes. The fruit is sliced and sun-dried, then powdered. Amchoor is pleasantly sour-tasting and used in northern Indian cooking to impart a sour flavor to dishes.

ANCHOVY Small fish, usually salted and canned with oil. Also available as paste. The product is salty.

APPLES The apples mentioned in this book are Golden Delicious and Granny Smith in 88 or 100 sizes.

ARTICHOKES Available fresh, frozen, or canned. Processed artichokes are sold as bottoms or as cleaned hearts.

ARUGULA   Salad green with a peppery, pungent flavor. Available in 4 oz (113 g) bunches. There is about 40 percent cleaning waste if stems are not used.

ASPIC   Jelly made with meat or fish flavor. It can be made from scratch and purchased in easy-to-use powder. Aspic is served with cold food as a component, and also is used to add a shining appearance to food to make it more appealing and to prevent drying out.

AVOCADOS   Available year round with peaks in fall and winter. There are two varieties—Hass with a rough, leathery skin (alligator pear) and Fuerte with a smooth skin. Avocados do not heat well and can become bitter when heated. Flavored avocado puree, called guacamole, is available canned and frozen with many different flavors.

BABY **VEGETABLES**   Available from specialty purveyors and normally sold by weight. Most common varieties of vegetables are available in tiny versions, the availability depends on season and location. Many baby vegetables are expensive. Exotic baby vegetables include tindora (bitter gourd), karela, and round eggplants. These vegetables tend to be bitter and should be slightly salted and refrigerated for 4 hours before use.

BACALAO DRIED COD   It is very salty and must be soaked before use. Large pieces, sold by weight, have fewer bones than smaller whole fish.

BAGUETTES   Thin, long breads with solid crust, often called flute, or just French bread. Available in most markets fresh. The diameter should be no more than 1½ in. (37 mm) to 2 in. (50 mm).

BALSAMIC VINEGAR   Aromatic wine vinegar which has been blended with grape juice and is then aged in wooden casks. The aging produces a mellow, mild product.

BASIL   Annual herb in the mint family with strong, pungent flavor. Available fresh in bunches and by weight.

BAY LEAVES   From the laurel tree, used for flavoring stocks. Fresh bay leaves from the Pacific Coast are narrower than the dried variety used for flavoring stock and are attractive as garnish. The stems can be used as skewers.

BEEF   The recipes in this book call for chopped meat and tenderloin. Chopped meat is prized according to fat content and the type of meat cut. Fat content of 20 percent is considered normal, although leaner meat is on the market. Chuck and round are the preferred cuts used for chopped meat. Tenderloin is best purchased completely cleaned and trimmed. It is often referred to by specification #190. A large tenderloin weighs about 5 to 6½ lb (2.25 to 3.00 kg), but they are available also as light as 3 lb (1.70 kg).

BEETS Available whole with greens still attached or canned, in slices or strips in various dimensions. Beets must be cooked before use. The color is strong and will dye anything it comes in contact with.

BESAN FLOUR, GRAM FLOUR Chick-pea flour, available in Indian stores.

BLUE CORN FLOUR Also called purple corn flour. Available in Hispanic stores under the name of *harina morada*.

BLUE CORNMEAL Coarse cornmeal made with blue corn.

BREAD Many varieties of breads are available in specialty stores as canape base. Many brands are available in small rounds or squares, and with interesting textures and flavors. Pepperidge Farms makes very thin sliced white bread. The bread is too thin as canape base, but suitable for baked sandwiches. Sandwich loaves #4 (referring to 4 x 4 in. slices (100 x 100 mm) are available from Fink Baking Corporation, Long Island City, New York.

BREAD CRUMBS Available commercially or made on premise by grinding stale bread. Softer and better crumbs are made with dense white bread, crust removed and chopped in the food processor.

BRUSSELS SPROUTS Vegetable in the cabbage family, available by weight or by pint. The trimming loss is about 30 percent. Frozen brussels sprouts can be substituted in some recipes.

BUCKWHEAT (KASHA) Cracked buckwheat normally sold in 1 lb (450 g) packages. 1 lb (450 g) is equivalent to about 2¼ cups (0.5 l).

BULGAR Cracked wheat.

BURDOCK Also called Gobo, it is a root vegetable common in Oriental cooking. The tender roots are peeled and cooked and can be grilled. They resemble salsify.

CABBAGE, **GREEN** Inexpensive vegetable, with two distinct varieties, summer and winter cabbage. Winter cabbage is firmer and whiter than summer cabbage.

CABBAGE, SAVOY Curly and soft cabbage, much milder than green cabbage. It will cook very quickly.

CAPE GOOSEBERRY (Also known as Chinese lantern, goldenberry, ground cherry, Peruvian cherry) Cherry-sized fruit, mustard gold in color and encased in a natural papery husk, with aromatic smell and medium sweet flavor. The fruit looks interesting and can be eaten raw. Available imported from mid-February to mid-June.

CAPERS Pungent buds of the Capparis plant, a shrub cultivated in Italy, Spain, and North Africa. Size is the major indication of quality, nonpareilles (nonparelles in Italian) are considered standard. Packed either in vinegar, which along with the plant's capric acid brings out the gherkin-like taste, or salted and dried.

CARAWAY SEED Spice related to anise, dill, and fennel, often used in European-style rye bread. The flavor is strong and the seeds have a tendency to get stuck between the teeth. It should be chopped by hand or in a machine.

CAVIAR Fish roe from a number of fish species, such as carp, lump fish, salmon, smelts, and sturgeon. Available fresh and pasteurized. Fresh caviar is lightly salted, is very perishable, and expensive. Pasteurized caviar is available in jars or cans. The most expensive caviar comes from the large beluga sturgeon; other sturgeon caviar is harvested from the sevruga and from osetra species. Red caviar comes from salmon, carp, or smelts. Lumpfish caviar is often dyed black and the color will stain other foods. Caviar should not be heated and should be always served very cold, even when in conjunction with a hot accompaniment.

CELERIAC Also known as celery root or root celery. A variety of celery with a bulb shaped root, 2½ to 4 in. (60 to 100 mm) across. Available in winter. The bulb must be peeled and should be kept in acidic water to avoid oxidation.

CELLOPHANE NOODLES Transparent noodles made of Mung Bean or other flour. Boil about 10 minutes or fry raw. Noodles will expand.

CÈPES See Mushrooms, dried.

CHAPATI FLOUR Whole wheat flour used in Indian breads.

CHEESES There are thousands of cheeses on the market. Only cheeses mentioned in the recipes (or substitutes) are listed here. Cheeses listed here are classified as grating cheeses, which do not melt when heated; cured cheeses that will melt; soft cheeses that need ripening; and fresh cheeses used in fillings or in dough recipes.

Cheeses which do not melt: Grating cheeses should pack as much flavor as possible. The best are made in Italy. Inexpensive domestic cheeses often have less flavor than Italian cheeses. Parmigiano Reggiano is the best of the wide variety of Parmesan cheeses. It is available in large wheels, or grated. The oldest is called stravecchio. Pecorino Romano is a grated cheese made with sheep's milk. Both Parmesan and Romano cheeses are available imported and domestically made. Sap Sago is made in Switzerland, comes in small cones, is green because of the addition of ground clover, and is hard to grate. Sbrinz is a Swiss grating cheese but only small quantities are exported. Domestic grating cheeses and imported cheeses from countries other than Italy are also on the market.

Cured cheeses that will melt: Cured mozzarella, mostly used for pizza. Available as whole milk cheese and part skim milk cheese. Swiss cheese has become a generic name and is made in many states and foreign countries. The genuine Swiss cheese comes from Switzerland and is called Emmenthal cheese; a close relative is Gruyère, made in Switzerland and in France. Norway makes a closely related cheese called Jarlsberg; Austria and Finland also export "Swiss Cheese." As a point of reference, imported cheese often has a stronger flavor than domestic cheese. Mangego cheese is from Spain and can be grated. Kefalograviera is a Greek semisoft cheese, excellent for deep frying. Available in Greek specialty stores. Cured cheeses should be diced or shredded when blended with a batter or paste. The mixture should be lukewarm to prevent the cheese from melting and getting stringy. Cheeses should not be subjected to high temperatures.

Blue cheeses that will melt are Blue d'Auvergne, Bleu de Bresse, and Roquefort made with sheep milk unique in flavor, from France; Danish Blue, white cheese with blue veins; Gorgonzola, made in Italy; Maytag, American made blue cheese; Stilton made in England with cow's milk, slightly salty. Blue cheese is normally saltier than other cheeses. The cheese mentioned do not melt evenly. Ripe cheese melt better than young cheese.

Soft cheeses that need to be ripened at room temperature. The flavor and aroma improves by the ripening process, at the same time the cheese will get soft and "runny," making handling difficult. Brie is available both domestically made and imported. It is one of the most popular soft dessert cheeses. The cheese is available in a number of flavors, such as herbs, peppercorns, and others. Camembert is closely related to Brie cheese. Boursin is a soft cheese from France.

Chèvre is the French name for goat and imported goat cheese is often referred to as Chèvre. Goat cheeses are made in a number of states and are also imported. Some imported cheeses are covered with a thin layer of ground wood cinders, which is edible. Goat cheeses come in different shapes. Bucheron is a French goat cheese in log shape.

Fresh cheese do not need ripening, must be kept under refrigeration, and should be used as soon as purchased. Fresh cheeses: Feta is a white cheese, made with goat's or cow's milk. It is sold in brine, and is slightly salty. Buffalo mozzarella is imported from Italy and is, in most instances, fresh. Fresh mozzarella is packed in brine and comes in different size balls. Ciliegine are small balls, bocconcino are bite-size balls.

Cream cheese is best purchased in 3 lb (1.3 kg) loaves. Baker's cheese is sold in 3 lb loaves and in tubs. Cottage cheese comes in 5 lb (2.25 kg) tubs.

CHESTNUTS Mild nut, rather sweet, available fresh, with skin on, during the winter. Peeled, dried chestnuts are also available. Edible only when cooked. Chestnuts can be cooked in a hot oven, in the microwave oven, or in the deep fryer until the skin pops and the nuts can be peeled. An incision to let steam escape must be made in the tough skins before they are cooked. Canned chestnuts are available in sugar syrup or plain, puree is also available sweetened and plain.

CHESTNUT FLOUR   Dried ground edible chestnuts. The flour can be used for thickening soups, but has limited use for baking because it has no gluten content.

CHICKEN BREAST   Boneless and skinless chicken breast is often called chicken cutlet. It is available fresh or frozen in many sizes, often sold in pairs—also called double breast. Common sizes for single breasts are 5 to 8 oz (140 to 225 g).

CHILIES   Chilies are available canned, dried, and fresh. Normally, the seeds are hotter than the flesh. Canned, peeled green Poblano chili is the mildest.

CHUTNEY   Sweet-sour condiment made with fruits and spices. The most common variety is made with mangos and is imported from India.

CILANTRO   The leafy greens of the coriander plant, often used in Mexican and Oriental cooking, also called Chinese parsley.

CLAMS   The clams used for the recipes in this book can be any type of hard shell (quahogs) clams. Fresh clams are available whole, shucked, and ground. Chowder clams are the biggest, cherrystones are medium size, and little necks are the smallest. Whole clams are hard to open without practice. Canned clams can be substituted.

COCONUTS   Shredded coconut meat is normally sold coated with sugar. If used in breading shrimp or other foods, it must be washed first and then dried. Unsweetened shredded coconut is available, but not carried by many purveyors.

CODFISH CHEEKS AND TONGUES   Old Yankee specialty available from specialty fish stores, although the diminishing catch of cod makes the items scarce. They need little cleaning.

CODFISH   Fresh cod can be purchased as Scrod when small, or as Market Cod, up to 8 lb (3.60 kg). Larger fish is less expensive than Scrod.

CORNICHON   French name for very small gherkins (pickles).

COUS-COUS   Semolina paste rolled into small granules and dried. The product can be used like pasta, but should be steamed rather than boiled. Instant Cous-Cous is mixed with hot water, cooked a few minutes, and is ready to use.

CRABMEAT   Available canned, fresh, or frozen in many quality levels. The best and most expensive is fresh lump crabmeat from the Atlantic Ocean, often referred to as Maryland crabmeat, followed by dungeness crabmeat from the Pacific. Alaskan crabmeat is available as King, the more expensive, and snow crabmeat, the less costly. When using fresh crabmeat it must be picked over to make sure all shells are removed. King and snow crabmeat come from large crabs and are normally free of shell particles.

CREAM   Cream is classified by butterfat content. Heavy cream has 36 percent or more fat, light cream has about 18 percent fat. Light cream will curdle when combined and boiled with an acidic ingredient; heavy cream will not.

CREAM PUFF PASTE   Also called puff paste or eclair paste. A soft paste which can be piped. The recipe is in Chapter 4, #R 107, page 44.

CRÈME DE MENTHE   Peppermint flavored sweet liquor available in green and white.

CREPES   Very thin pancakes. They can be purchased frozen, ready to use, or made fresh. Frozen crepes are often sweetened and not suitable for hors d'oeuvres.

CUMIN   Distinctive spice powder used in Hispanic and Middle Eastern cooking.

DAIKON   Large, white Oriental radish. Available in most Oriental vegetable stores in many sizes. Daikon sprouts make attractive garnishes.

DASHI   Japanese clear soup made with dried bonito flakes. Bonito flakes are available in Oriental food stores. Directions for use are often on the package.

DATES   Fresh dates are seldom available on the market. They are in season September and October. When purchasing dried dates, specify pitted and sun-dried.

DOILY, DOILIES   Cloth or paper articles used for two purposes in food service. One is to prevent sliding when one piece of china, silver, or glassware is put on top of another. The second purpose is to soak up fat when fried food is served. Cloth doilies should be made of lint-free absorbent cotton. Paper doilies come in two varieties, glassine and absorbent. The absorbent variety can be solid or lace. All doilies come in many shapes and colors. The use of doilies is somewhat old-fashioned, but needed to prevent sliding. In food service, doilies are not decorative items to be used indiscriminately.

DRIED APRICOTS   Available in bulk and in 1 lb (450 g) packages. The sizes range from jumbo to #6, which is a standard size.

DRIED CRANBERRIES   Available by weight.

DRIED SOUR CHERRIES   Available by weight. Note that candied cherries are sweet and are not suitable for hors d'oeuvres recipes.

DRIED MANGO   Called amchoor in India. Raw mango, dried and ground. The powder is acidic and is used as spice.

DULSE   Protein- and iron-rich sea vegetable available dried. Slightly chewy and salty. Can be eaten as purchased or cooked.

EGG ROLL SKINS   Also called Wonton skin or spring roll skins. They can be purchased ready to use. The most common package contains 14 wrappers about 6 in. (150 mm) square. To seal wrapper properly, make paste with 6 parts water and 2 parts flour or cornstarch.

ESCARGOTS   Snails, practically always sold canned. There are about 36 Extra Large size snails, or 48 very large snails in a 9 oz (250 g) can.

FILO   Also spelled phyllo Very thin dough sheets, normally sold frozen or fresh in 1 lb (450 g) packages. There are about 20 each sheets 12 x 17 in. (300 x 425 mm), medium thickness, in a package. The dough will dry very quickly when exposed to air and must always be covered with a moist (not wet) towel during use.

FINNAN   Haddie Smoked haddock fillets, available in fillets fresh or frozen. Some product is only cured and colored, not smoked, and has inferior flavor. The product can be salty and should be poached in milk/water mixture to dilute the salt flavor.

FLOUR   Wheat Flour is generally divided into strong flour and soft flour. Strong has a high gluten content and is used for pasta and bread baking, the most commonly used is called bread flour. Soft flour is called cake flour and is used in making cakes and pies. Four cups bread flour, sifted, weigh 1 lb (450 g); 4½ to 5 cups cake flour weigh 1 lb (450 g). Flour should always be weighed because volume measurement is unreliable.

FOIE GRAS   French for fatty liver. Goose or duckling livers from specially raised birds are available fresh in some markets, but most likely made into paté or spreads. The price depends on whether the liver is used whole or is chopped, whether truffles are included, and on the amount of other ingredients, mostly other livers or meats. The name block refers to whole liver, *mousse* indicates a spread. *Terrine* is a reference to the container it was cooked in, although it is also sold in cans. Read the label carefully. The product is expensive.

FRESH PASTA, PASTA SKINS Available in many flavors, precooked or raw.

271

GALANGAL   Aromatic roots are also called Siamese ginger, sold dried in slices, fresh and powdered.

GARBANZOS   Called chickpeas. The product is available canned, dried, fresh, and frozen. Canned Garbanzos are practical to use.

GELATIN   Flavorless gelatin is available in sheets and in powder form. The powdered gelatin is easier to use than sheet gelatin. Gelatin sheets must be soaked in cold water, before being added to a hot liquid. 1 oz (28 g) thickens (solidifies) about 2 qt (1.85 l) liquid.

GHERKINS   Small pickles, available sweet or acidic, often flavored with dill seeds.

GINGER, PICKLED   Shredded product, normally dyed red, and preserved in vinegar and salt. Available in Oriental stores.

GINGER, FRESH   Rinzone, available by weight. Wrinkled skin indicates old product. Purchase large, relatively even pieces. The vegetable must be peeled and cut across the fibers, then it can be diced or chopped. Pickled ginger is available in Oriental stores.

GOOSE LIVER (FOIE GRAS)   See Foie gras.

GRAPES   Seedless grapes are available red or green all year. Sold by weight or in lugs.

GRAPE LEAVES   Available pickled in brine. The leaves are very salty and should be soaked before use.

GRAVE LAX   Scandinavian method for curing salmon. The recipe is in Chapter 4, #R 178, page 78.

HAM, PROSCIUTTO   The word is generic Italian for ham, but is used for air-dried ham, eaten uncooked. When heated, the ham can be rather tough and salty. It must be sliced very thin. Prosciutto is available imported and domestically made. The boneless version is convenient to use.

HAM, CURED   Cured ham is available in many versions, quality levels, and shapes. The ham mentioned in most recipes should be ready to eat, and contain little fat and added water.

HAM, VIRGINIA Lean ham from peanut-fed hogs which is cured and very slowly dry smoked. It is then coated with ground pepper. The ham is saltier than regular ham and requires soaking before boiling. The meat is rather dry. It is best purchased boneless fully cooked/baked. Imitation "Virginia Style" ham is baked ham with a sweet glaze and does not compare with the genuine Virginia ham.

HARUSAME NOODLES Noodles that puff up when fried. Attractive breading for fried food. Available in Oriental stores.

HAZELNUTS Also called Filberts, although there is a botanical difference between the two. The nuts are best purchased in cans shelled and peeled. Roasting brings out the nutty flavor.

HOISIN SAUCE Sweetish sauce made from pumpkin. Available canned or bottled in Oriental stores.

HORSERADISH Pungent root, available fresh or grated in vinegar, sometimes mixed with beets. It should not be boiled.

JERUSALEM ARTICHOKE Also called *tobinambour,* root vegetable with mild flavor native to the Americas. It can be boiled like potatoes.

JICAMA Large white root, also called Mexican potato, but unlike the potato it can be eaten raw.

KANPYO Oriental dried gourd strings. Available in packages in Oriental stores.

KELP Seaweed available fresh, dried, and ground. Powdered kelp can be used as salt substitute. Dried kelp, called *konbu* in Japanese, looks like dark leather strips.

KOHLRABI Also called cabbage turnip. Vegetable consisting of a bulb growing above ground, about 2 to 3 in. (50 to 75 mm) across. It should be precooked and is delicious grilled. Large size kohlrabi are often woody.

LAMB'S LETTUCE Also called by the French name mache. Very early spring lettuce with tiny leaves and slightly bitter flavor.

LEMONGRASS A tropical grass resembling leeks with pleasant lemon aroma. The lower white part is edible. Available dried, fresh, and powdered. Dried lemongrass can be reconstituted by soaking it in water.

LENTIL   Dried lentils are available in a number of colors, ranging from gray/brown to orange. The flavor varies little. They cook in about 1 hour.

LOTUS ROOT   The fresh bulbs are sold by weight and are a string of several grayish bulbs about 4 x 8 in. (100 x 200 mm). The cut root will oxidize unless kept in acidic water.

LOX   Cured salmon from large, fatty fish. The name is used sometimes erroneously for smoked salmon. It is cheaper than smoked salmon and can be ground for use in fillings.

LICHEES   Oriental fruit served pitted and canned. Lychee nuts are the same fruit, but dried. They are not nuts. Fresh lichees are grown in Florida and are in season June and July.

MANGO   Kidney-shaped fruit with large pit and fibrous flesh. Mangoes vary greatly in size. The fruit is green when unripe, yellow and soft when ripe. Green mango is an interesting fruit which can be grilled.

MASA HARINA   Instant cornmeal treated with lime, made in the United States by Quaker Oats Company for Mexican dishes, especially tamales.

MASALA PASTE OR POWDER   Curry-like Indian spice available in many degrees of hot (spiciness) and flavor combinations.

MINT   Perennial herb with many variations. Available fresh all year.

MINT JELLY   Green jelly based on apple juice and mint flavor.

MIRIN   Japanese sweet rice beer.

MISO/MISO PASTE JAPANESE   A paste of fermented soybeans used to thicken and season soups, marinades, and sauces. Available in a wide variety of flavors, colors, and textures, but basically classified as aka (red miso), dark brown and pungent, chu (golden miso) is mild, and shiro (white or tan miso), is slightly sweet. Miso paste is perishable and should be kept refrigerated. It will not freeze. Miso has a very high salt content. The miso used in this book is chu (golden miso).

MOLE   Mexican seasoning containing bitter chocolate. The dish with the same name originated in the city of Puebla and involved extensive preparation of blending spices and ingredients. Mole is now available as powder and paste. Some is rather spicy and should be used with caution. The color is dark brown.

MOO-SHU SHELLS (wrappers or doilies)   Thin pancakes, but made with a solid dough rather than with a batter. Peking duck is always served with moo-shu. Available in most Chinese grocery stores.

MUSHROOMS, DRIED   Many varieties of mushrooms are available dried. The most flavorful are porcini, often imported from Italy, called cèpes in French, and Steinpilze in German. Other varieties are chanterelles, morels, and Oriental mushrooms. Dried mushrooms have an intense flavor which will enhance meat and vegetable fillings. They should be soaked before use and boiled in the same water they were soaked in. Inexpensive morels imported from India and Pakistan have a smoky flavor because they could have been dried over cow dung fire. Dried mushrooms come in different quality levels.

MUSHROOMS, FRESH, WILD   Morels and chanterelles are the best known varieties. Sold by weight.

MUSHROOMS, FRESH, CULTIVATED   Mushrooms are sold by weight. White or brown champignon is the most common mushroom. Cremini mushrooms are the forerunners of the common cultivated mushrooms. Enoki mushrooms, also called Snow Puff Mushrooms, look like an enlarged pin. They have a long skinny stem, about 3 or 4 in. (75 to 100 mm) in length, and a tiny round head or cap. They have almost no taste, but make a great appearance. They are common decorations in Japanese cuisine. Pleurotes, also known as golden trumpets because of their shape and color, are from an Indian strain. The American varieties come trimmed, with or without the stalk. The American pleurotes are usually not as large as the Italian ones. As they become larger, they exude more spores, making them difficult for pickers because of allergic reactions. Portobello or Roman mushrooms are actually the same mushroom as Cremini, but left to mature longer in the field. As they mature, they become flatter and the flavor intensifies. When cooking with them, it is advisable to use an acid such as lemon juice, to avoid the very dark color that the mushrooms will otherwise exude.

MUSSELS   Available fresh and canned. Farmed mussels have basically no grit and are easy to use. Some cultivated mussels are quite large; for hors d'oeuvres use 10 to 14 pieces to a pound.

MUSTARD   The product is available as powder, often called English mustard, and prepared in countless variations. Prepared mustard used in the recipes should be of good quality, not too sharp, and without grain. Powdered mustard is very pungent and must be mixed with a little water to a paste. Mustard should not be cooked.

NORI   Also called laver, is a type of sea vegetation marketed as thin, dried sheets. The best quality is black; green sheets are made with an inferior type of sea vegetables. The sheets are 6 x 10 in. (150 x 250 mm) and are pliable, but will dissolve when wet. They are best rolled on a bamboo mat. Laver sheets should be toasted over an open flame to develop flavor. There are many varieties of nori available in Oriental grocery stores.

OATMEAL   Available as quick cooking or regular. Stone ground oats are considered superior to regular oatmeal.

OIL   The basic distinction is between neutral, almost flavorless oils and oils that have a specific flavor. Flavorless oils are commercial cooking oils, basically a medium to transfer heat and cook food. Flavored oils are olive oils in many flavor levels, oils made from sesame seeds used in Oriental cooking, palm oil, and oils that have been flavored with herbs and spices. Unless specified, oil mentioned in the recipes is neutral, commercial oil. Olive oil can range from very flavorful cold pressed virgin oil, often pale green, to commercial quality oils made by extracting all oil from the olives with chemicals.

OLIVES, GREEN   Available pickled, whole, pitted, or stuffed.

OLIVES, BLACK   Available as domestic canned olives in many sizes, whole or pitted. These olives have been treated to be black and have a bland taste. Imported black olives are ripe olives, pickled and often sold in brine or in oil, also salted and dried. Their flavors vary, and some are rather strong for the average taste.

PANCETTA   Italian bacon normally not smoked, but also available smoked from Northern Italy.

PAPA CRIOLLA   Generic name for unusual potatoes used in South American cooking. The color can range from blue to yellow, and the potatoes are normally rather small and round.

PAPRIKA   Ground spice made from dried red peppers. The market distinguishes between Spanish and Hungarian paprika. Spanish paprika has less flavor than Hungarian paprika and is often less expensive. Hungarian paprika is sold in varying degrees of sharpness. The normal paprika is called sweet.

PARSLEY   There are two varieties–curly parsley and flat leaf, also called Italian parsley. The flavor of Italian parsley is stronger than the flavor of curly parsley. Curly parsley chops better and gives more bulk when chopped.

PASSION FRUIT Also called Grenadilla, a purple-skinned tropical fruit with yellow flesh and edible seeds.

PASTRAMI Cured, smoked beef covered with crushed coriander seeds. The best cuts are made from plate and weigh about 2 lb (900 g). Available fully cooked or precooked.

PEARS Available year round. Pears are harvested while still hard and are ripened under controlled conditions. Once ripe they will get overripe rapidly. Ripening can be done at room temperature. The most common varieties are Anjou, with a brown skin and firm flesh and Bartlett, purchased green, and yellow when ripe. Comice pears are in season in winter. They are large, juicy pears with a gritty taste.

PEPPER White and black pepper are available ground and whole. Butcher ground pepper is coarse ground black pepper.

PEPPERCORNS Available black and white. White peppercorns are made by grinding off the dark outer layer. Unripe peppercorns are sold as pink, red, and green, either dried or pickled in brine and vinegar.

PERNOD Licorice (anise) flavored alcoholic beverage imported from France. Other Anise flavored brandies can be substituted.

PESTO Mixture of basil, garlic, oil, pine nuts, and Romano cheese. Ready pesto is available. The best product is made by Casa Di Lisio in Mt. Kisco, New York.

PINE NUTS Also called pignoli nuts, the soft, oval kernels are available peeled in vacuum cans. They should be roasted before use to bring out the full flavor.

PINEAPPLE Available in 4, 5, 6, and 7 counts per half box. Peak is in April and May. Ripe pineapples are seldom available away from the growing area.

PLANTAIN, PLATEN Cooking banana, available in different shades from green and very hard to yellow and soft, but it cannot be eaten raw, even when soft and ripe. Best purchased slightly yellow and firm. The product gets sweeter as it matures. Available by weight and piece. The average piece weighs 10 to 14 oz (280 to 390 g).

POLENTA Cornmeal, cooked to a mush. The best cornmeal is available in ethnic markets, such as Hispanic, Italian, or Hungarian, because the product is coarser than the cornmeal sold as breakfast cereal.

POMEGRANATE Tropical fruit. Grenadine syrup is made with this fruit.

POPPY SEED Grayish/black seeds, rather fatty and should be kept refrigerated. The seeds are used in baking. Ground boiled and sweetened seeds are used as pastry fillings.

PORK TENDERLOIN   Thin muscle available fresh or frozen. The average weight is about 8 to 10 oz (225 to 280 g). There is some skin and fat that still has to be removed, and the muscle is tapered toward the tip.

POTATOES   There are basically two types of potatoes–waxy potatoes and mealy potatoes, called Russet. In this book Russet potatoes are used. These potatoes are often called Idaho or baking potatoes and are sold graded by shape and size. An average size is 80 pieces to a carton. The exact sizes are indicated in the recipes.

PUFF PASTE DOUGH   Dough made with water and flour, into which many layers of fat or butter are incorporated. Can be purchased frozen in sheets. Making the dough is an elaborate process which requires a cold room and a dough rolling machine.

QUAIL **EGGS**   Available fresh and canned, boiled.

QUAIL   Small birds, farm raised and available completely eviscerated. They should weigh about 5 to 6 oz (140 to 170 g). Split, frozen quail are also available.

QUINOA   Grain originally from the Andes with high protein content.

RICE **WAFER PAPER**   Thin sheets, about 8½ x 11 in. (212 to 250 mm), brittle and completely edible. When slightly moistened, the sheets become pliable and can be used to wrap soft fillings. However, when the sheets are wet, they will dissolve.

RICE, ARBORIO   Short grain, polished Italian rice, translucent with an opaque center that becomes somewhat glutinous when cooked. It is most commonly used to make risotto.

RICE, OKOME   Short-grain rice, grown for Japanese cooking. The best known California grown brands are California Rose, Blue Rose, or Calrose. This rice is used for sushi, rice cakes, and as side dishes.

ROSEMARY   Perennial herb, growing in temperate climate to small scrub size. The needles and stems are very aromatic and can be fried or roasted whole.

SAFFRON   Expensive spice. Genuine saffron is imported from Spain and Greece. Imitation saffron is available from Mexico. Whole saffron is better than ground saffron. Allow whole saffron to steep in liquid to get better flavor extraction.

SAKE   Japanese rice beer with about 18 percent alcohol content, served warm.

SALMON   Fish available all year, because it is extensively farmed in many parts of the world. There are many species, but for the purpose of this book, bright red color is an important consideration. King salmon, also called chinook, and sockeye salmon and farmed-raised Norwegian salmon have very red flesh. Available in many sizes, whole, headless and gutted (dressed), as fillets and loins; completely boneless loins are expensive and are useful when small quantities are needed.

SALSIFY   Also called oyster plant, this vegetable resembles white asparagus in shape and parsnip in flavor when cooked. It is available fresh and canned, it can be grilled when parboiled.

SAUSAGE CASING   Available as salted natural casings or as manufactured casing from specialty butcher shops. Salted casings must be soaked, and the water changed a number of times to remove the salt. Casings keep well in water in the refrigerator.

SAVORY   Herb, seldom available fresh. It is used to flavor game and vegetables.

SCALLOPS, BAY   Edible mollusk, the muscle (foot) about ½ in (13 mm) across, sold fresh by the gallon or frozen by weight.

SCALLOPS, SEA   Large mollusk, with a muscle (foot) up to 2 in (50 mm) across. The count is about 160–240 pieces per gallon.

SCALLOPS IN THE SHELL   Specialty item now available, with the roe still attached. The scallops are attractive and very practical for hors d'oeuvres because they can be broiled and served directly with the shell. However, they are expensive.

SCONES   Baking powder biscuits of English origin. They can be baked or griddle fried.

SESAME LEAVES   Attractive leaves available in Oriental stores. They can be eaten raw.

SESAME OIL   Aromatic oil used in Oriental dishes. The oil is a flavor ingredient, not a cooking oil.

SESAME SEEDS   Available black and white. They should be toasted lightly to increase flavor, unless used in an ingredient which is exposed to direct heat.

SHALLOTS Small bulbs in the onion family with mild flavor. There are 40–50 large shallots in 1 lb (450 g), or 20–25 jumbo shallots in 1 lb (450 g).

SHERRY Fortified wine with about 18 percent alcohol content, available dry, semidry, and sweet. The wine originated in Spain, but imitation sherry is made in many countries.

SHISO LEAVES The green leaves are used in tea and are an attractive garnish with Japanese dishes. The plant, also called beefsteak plant, grows in moderate climate.

SHRIMP Shrimp are fished in most parts of the oceans and come in many sizes and quality levels. There are three principal kinds of shrimp—white, pink, and brown.

Large shrimp are often called Prawns. Price is dependent on size. Pink shrimp are considered most desirable in food service. Shrimp are shipped frozen, except in local markets. Shrimp with the head left on are becoming available and can be quite attractive. Farmed shrimp constitute a major share of the market and are popular in food service because the center intestine is invisible and does not have to be removed. Tiger shrimp are farmed shrimp with an attractive shell.

Headless Shrimp Headless shrimp, often called green shrimp, in the shell, with the head removed. They are sold on the basis of count per 1 lb (450 g). The most common sizes are under 8, under 10, 10–15, 16–20, 21–25, 26–30, 31–35.

P&D shrimp are peeled and deveined. They are normally shipped as individually quick-frozen shrimp, also referred to as IQF. In order to prevent freezer burns, they are coated, or glazed with water. P&D shrimp are available by count per pound, or as broken pieces, sold by weight. Broken pieces can be used for recipes calling for ground shrimp.

SMOKED SALMON The product is available in many sizes, quality levels, and packs. Some products are imported. Available are sides (halves) with the skin on, whole or presliced or skin off whole or sliced. Unsliced salmon sides must be boned.

Average sizes range for North American sides from 3 to 6 lb (1.35 kg to 2.70 kg). Imported sides are normally smaller. For the uses intended in this book it is best to buy whole sides, about 5 to 6 lb (2.25 to 2.70 kg), cut in chunks as indicated in the recipes. Chill and slice on the electric meat slicer into thin sheets.

SMOKED SHAD A migratory fatty fish caught in spring. The fish is very bony and only fillets should be purchased. A fillet is about 8 to 12 oz (225 g to 335 g).

SMOKED TROUT The product is available whole, head on, and in boneless fillets. Product is sometimes frozen.

SMOKED WHITEFISH The product is available whole, head on. The fish is very bony. Small smoked whitefish is called chub. Fresh smoked whitefish is a wonderful product, but when frozen the product can be watery and lose much flavor.

SORREL (SOUR GRASS) Green weed with very acidic taste. As soon as the vegetable is cooked it will turn gray due to its natural acidity. The weed has a very high water content and must be well strained before use. Sorrel is often used in soups for flavor.

SOY SAUCE Available now in light and dark and with reduced salt content. Japanese soy sauce is lighter than Chinese sauce.

SPAGHETTI SQUASH Winter squash, although available year round, with hard shell. It should be split and baked or boiled, and the stringy flesh, resembling spaghetti, can be removed with a spoon. The flesh can also be scraped out of the shell while still raw.

SPINACH, FRESH There are two basic varieties—curly leaf spinach, called savoy and flat leaf spinach, called broad-leaf spinach. The curly leaf savoy spinach ships better than the flat leaf spinach. Semi-savoy spinach is occasionally available. Loose spinach is shipped both clipped, with some stems removed, and in bunches. Small amounts are best purchased in trimmed cello pack, to ready to cook, unless large leaves are needed. In this case spinach in bunches should be purchased.

SPINACH, FROZEN Available whole leaf, chopped, and IQF (individually quick frozen).

STAR FRUIT Often called carambola. A 4 in. (100 mm) long tropical fruit which is star shaped when cut across. The yellow variety, also called star apple, can be eaten raw when ripe. The green variety, also called tree cucumber, must be cooked.

STRUDEL Austrian/German word for a rolled baked item resembling a snake. Strudel in Austria is often made with thin filo dough; in Germany and Switzerland with puff pastry. The fillings can vary from fruits and sweet cream cheese to spinach, meats, and other cheeses. The best known strudel is the apple strudel.

SUN-DRIED TOMATOES Tomato halves which have been dehydrated. They pack a lot of flavor. They are available dry, and packed in oil, in many price categories. Important is the flavor level, which can vary greatly. Dried product should be soaked before most applications.

SUNFLOWER SEEDS Available shelled and slightly salted in health food stores.

SURIMI Seafood substitute made with inexpensive fish, flavored and shaped to resemble crabmeat, shrimp, and lobster. It is acceptable as filling material, but should never be sold as the real product.

SUSHI VINEGAR (SUSHI SU)   Mild vinegar made from rice.

SWEETBREADS   See Veal sweetbreads.

TAHINI PASTE   Paste made with ground sesame seeds, available in Middle Eastern and Oriental stores.

TAMARIND   Large brown bean pods with sour flavor. It is available as paste or juice in Indian stores.

TAMARI SAUCE   Aged soy sauce, milder than regular soy sauce.

TEARDROP TOMATOES   Small tomato, smaller than cherry tomatoes, shaped like drops. Available in red and yellow from specialty produce houses.

TEMPEH   Fermented soybean cake of Indonesian origin.

TERRINE   Ceramic container to cook slowly in the oven, it is also the name of the food, which is almost always served cold. A terrine of salmon, for example, is salmon mousse.

THYME   Herb with strong flavor, good with beef dishes. Available fresh. The leaves are very small, the stems are woody.

TOFU   Unfermented soybean paste available in Oriental grocery stores. The consistency varies greatly, from soft to rather solid. Tofu is normally sold by weight in small blocks, stored in brine.

TOMATO PRODUCTS   Tomato products are available in variations too numerous to list. Tomato puree is thinner and lighter than tomato paste.

TOMATILLO   Also called jam-berry. Native fruit from Mexico, looks like a large yellow cherry in a paper-like husk.

TORTILLA, FLOUR   Widely available in many sizes from 6 to 16 in. (250 to 400 mm).

TORTILLA, CORN   Available in many sizes.

TRITICALE   Grain, cross between wheat and rye with high gluten content.

TRUFFLES   Very expensive mushrooms that grow underground in France and Italy. Some truffles are also found in other countries. Although the truffle fungus is abundant, edible truffles are very scarce and are not yet cultivated. The white Italian truffle is in season November/December and the black French truffle is in season December to March. Italian summer truffles are available from May to October, but lack the intense flavor of the other truffles. Truffles are available mostly canned as whole truffle, chopped and as chopped peelings. Truffles are luxury items and will increase the food cost considerably.

TRUFFLE BUTTER   Butter mix flavored with truffle extract. It will give some truffle flavor to food, but not color.

TURMERIC   Ground root used as spice, as yellow dyes, and as an important ingredient in curry powder.

TUNA   Large ocean fish with dark, sometimes oily meat that will lighten after cooking.

There are many varieties; bluefin is the largest with specimens weighing up to 600 lb (270 kg). Tuna is one of the most popular fish varieties in sushi bars.

UDAD   Also called papadoms. Indian flat bread made with legume flour. It comes in dried disks about 6 in. (150 mm) across and must be fried or toasted before use. Available plain and with different spices and seeds. Some versions can be very hot.

VARK   Edible gold or silver foil. It is very thin and is sold between layers of tissue paper. Available in Indian grocery stores.

VEAL SWEETBREADS   The thymus gland of young animals. Veal sweetbreads are lighter in color than calf's sweetbreads. Sweetbread pairs consist of two uneven parts. They are often sold separated.

WALNUTS   Available shelled, whole or in pieces.

WASABE   Japanese horseradish, normally sold in powdered form, when mixed with water will make a strong, green paste.

WATER CHESTNUTS   Available canned, fresh, and also as flour. In Oriental cooking, a number of different varieties are clearly distinguished. Fresh water chestnuts are available only in ethnic markets. The canned product is the accepted food service standard. Canned water chestnuts are available sliced or whole. Fresh water chestnuts are brown bulbs with white interior.

WATERCRESS   Available by the bunch.

WILD RICE   The price differences in wild rice are based on the amount of broken kernels. For fritters, a blend of 50 percent or more broken pieces is adequate.

WINE LEAVES   Available in jars, pickled in brine. The leaves should be washed or soaked before being stuffed.

WINE   Wine used for cooking should be flavorful and have a good color. White wine should not be sweet, because it is often reduced and therefore the sweetness is increased. Wine should be of good quality, but should not be expensive. Jug wine is normally adequate. Cooking wine is seasoned with salt and should not be used.

WONTON SKINS   See Egg roll skins. Also called spring roll skins.

YAMA GOBO   Pickled burdock, available in Oriental grocery stores.

ZUCCHINI   Green summer squash available by weight. Small, firm squash should be purchased, because larger zucchini can be spongy.

Cooking Terms

In order to shorten the recipes and to avoid misunderstanding, the cooking terms used in this book are explained.

Batter	Pourable mixture consisting of starches, fillers, binding, and sometimes of leavening agents.
Blend	Combine carefully
Blind bake	Line mold with dough, cover dough with foil, and fill cavity with dried legumes or other suitable material to prevent dough from sliding into the cavity during baking.
Boil	Cook in liquid at 212°F/100°C.
Dice	Cut in squares; the sizes can vary greatly.
Dip	Insert solid food into a liquid mixture.
Dough	Pliable mixture of starches and other ingredients.
Dust	Sprinkle flour on table or into pans to prevent dough from sticking to surface.
Egg wash	Mixture of equal parts milk or light cream and eggs, to be brushed on products before baking.
Fold	Mix gently as not to break air bubbles in the mixture or create air bubbles.
Julienne	French term for food cut into thin strips about match size.
Marinades	Aromatic and acidic mixture to soak meat and other food for preservation and to impart flavors.
Measuring cup	Container with scale indicating fluid ounce content of liquid or solid food.
Mix	Combine various ingredients.
Mousse	Light, fluffy food, can be served hot or cold, sweet or meat, and fish based.
Poach	Cook in liquid below boiling point at about 200°F/95°C or below.
Profiterole	French term for small cream puff.
Puff paste	Also called cream puff paste or pâte à chou. Soft boiled dough that can be piped and then fried or baked.

Puff paste dough   Also called pâte (pâte feuilletée). Dough consisting of layers of fat (butter or margarine). The dough will be flaky when baked.

Scale   Indispensable measuring devise in baking and other food production.

Slice   Cut with knife or electric slicing machine.

Steam   Cook in closed container in gaseous water above 212°F/100°C.

Wash   Paint surface of dough with egg mixture, milk, or other liquids to enhance flavor and encourage even coloring during baking.

tbsp   Tablespoon, or one 16th of a cup.

tsp   Teaspoon, or one third of a tablespoon.

Equipment Descriptions Mentioned in This Book

There is much labor-saving equipment on the market, and we assume that most operations are equipped with basic equipment.

Buffets are theater productions and appropriate equipment and props are an integral part of the display. The equipment consists of food service equipment, such as display platters, bowls, chafing dishes, cutting boards, and props which set the mood for the party. Large banquet houses have props, such as statues, fountains, shells, carts, boats, and risers in stock. In some cases the props take up much room, making it difficult to access the food, and very hard to get it maintained and resupplied. However, the public loves it.

Ice sculptures have a special niche on the market. In most locations ice sculptures can be purchased from a local supplier if there is no in house talent. Ice sculptures can also be made with plastic molds.

Following is the most common equipment mentioned in this book:

Bain marie Water bath

baskets Wire baskets to deep food in boiling water for blanching should be round and are available in a number of sizes. Wicker baskets for table decoration and for food display come in many shapes and sizes.

broiler Cooking device with the heat source from the top. It can be gas or electrically heated. A broiler is not essential in a catering operation, but can be handy to brown food (including desserts) and to toast large amounts of bread efficiently.

chafing dish Buffet equipment to keep food warm in a water bath. It can be heated with alcohol, canned heat, or with electricity. Canned heat is available as paste or in closed containers with wicks.

chopsticks Pair of wood, plastic, or metal sticks, the standard eating utensils in the Orient. The sticks are handy when dipping food in batter, and have many other uses.

compotier French word for cake or cookie stand.

dippers Large ladles, or pots with long handles, to transfer liquids efficiently.

food processor One of the most important kitchen machines. For many years food processors were only available in large sizes and limited to commercial kitchens. Now food processors are available in many sizes and are indispensable in any kitchen.

French knife
Better called Chef's knife, because it is made in many countries. It is important that the knife has a solid blade, is well balanced, and either stays sharp or can be sharpened easily. The handle can be made of wood or plastic.

garnishing bag
Also called pastry bag. It is made of plastic material and is available in many sizes. Garnishing bags can harbor harmful bacteria and should be boilable.

griddle
A cooking device with a polished steel top; it can be heated electrically or with gas. Griddles comes in many sizes and are very practical pieces of equipment for the caterer.

grill
Cooking equipment consisting of a grid or parallel rods with a heat source underneath. The source can be gas, electricity, or wood embers.

grinder
If the table mixer (see *mixer*) is not equipped with a powerful motor, a table model meat grinder is useful. It should have at least one coarse, one medium, and one very fine plate.

kettle
Kettles are very handy when liquid must be heated. Kettles come in all sizes, from large floor mounted kettles to table size trunion kettles. All are steam jacket kettles. Large kettles need a steam generating boiler; small table kettles, also called trunion kettles, can be self-contained and heated by electricity. There are basically three types; smooth sided tilting kettles for sauces and stews, stationary kettles with drains, and tilting kettles with drains. Each kettle has specific uses and applications. For catering operations tilting kettles with drains are probably the most practical choice. Important are well located floor drains and a nearby water faucet.

knives
Beside French knives in at least two sizes, other knives indispensable in cooking include paring knives and slicers. Paring knives should be small, and have a solid blade. Slicers should have a wide blade. Items often forgotten in off-premise catering situations are knives, and it is advisable to have at least one extra set in the truck.

ladles
Ladles are available in sizes from ½ oz (0.015 l) to 32 oz (0.92 l). It is important that the handle is long and flat to provide a sure grip, and solidly riveted to the cup. Cheap ladles have a short handle.

mandolin	Hand-operated slicer with different built-in blades. It is a useful piece of equipment, but much work accomplished by a mandolin can be done much faster with a food processor with appropriate attachment blades or with an electric slicer.
measuring cups	Essential in catering operations. There should be a number of 1 cup, 2 cups, quart, and gallon measures.
melon baller	Available in many sizes. Scooped out fruits are somewhat old-fashioned but melon ballers are very useful to scoop out vegetables or the core of apples or pears.
mixer	Electric mixers are available in many sizes, starting with 1 qt (.92 l) table models to large floor models. The size selected depends on the scope of intended catering, but the capacity of the bowl should be large enough to make the average amount of batter at one time. There should always be at least one extra bowl. There should be whips, paddles for making medium soft batters, and dough hooks for making stiff dough. Most mixers come with a grinder attachment, which is useful only if the motor is strong.
mixing bowls	There can never be too many bowls in all sizes. They should be made of stainless steel.
molds	Molds are rather inexpensive and there should be many sizes and shapes available. Nonstick molds are handy, but expensive. Very small brioche molds are hard to find.
muffin tins	The very small muffin tins are hard to find, but are essential when making muffins for hors d'oeuvres.
nonstick pans	This type of cookware is very handy for making fillings and for frying fritters. It is important to remember that this cookware will scratch easily. Only nonmetal spoons or spatulas should be used.
paddle	Wood or metal utensil available in many sizes. It is useful when making heavy pastes, such as cream puff paste, or corn meal mush.
pastry bag	See *garnishing bag*.
pastry table	The pastry table should have a hardwood top and the legs should be brazed to provide a solid foundation. If the pastry table is placed against the wall, it should be provided with a backsplash. The table must be carefully maintained; it should never be used for chopping or for any other use. If the table must be used for another purpose, it

should be covered with paper to protect the surface. Hardwood pastry tables seldom need scrubbing with water; in most instances the table can be cleaned with a pastry broom and kitchen towels.

Marble topped tables are only practical when large amounts of pastries or sugar items are produced. In most cases a small marble slab is adequate for most applications.

pastry brush   There should be a number of brushes, some for fat and others for nonfat applications. It is best to purchase brushes with handles with two different colors. Brushes sold in hardware stores work well. It must be remembered that bristles cannot be exposed to heat, because they will melt or burn.

pastry tubes   These tubes are used with the pastry/garnishing bag. Smooth tubes are considered essential, garnishes made with star tubes are considered old-fashioned.

peeler   A number of good peelers are handy and not expensive. The standard model with a metal handle works well. When a peeler is no longer sharp it should be discarded.

range   See *stoves*.

ravier(s)   French word for glass or china serving dish(s) used for cold appetizers. Six to eight raviers are presented on a platter and each ravier holds a number of servings.

roasting pans   These pans should be made of black iron. They will rust if stored wet.

rolling pin   There are two basic types of rolling pins. One is referred to as "French pin" and consists or a stick dowel, about 2 in. (50 mm) thick. In some cases the pin is also tapered on both sides. The other type of rolling pin has handles on both sides. The better quality pins have roller bearings. Rolling pins should not be immersed in hot water. Cleaning with a moist kitchen towel is sufficient.

salamander   Cooking device with a heat source overhead. Smaller models or often called "cheese melters." If a broiler is available a salamander is not needed, but if there is no broiler, a small wall-mounted electric unit can be rather handy.

scale   A catering operation should have at least three scales. One scale is to check incoming merchandise. In most operations a table size scale for up to 25 lb (11.25 kg) is sufficient. Electronic scales are convenient, but expensive. The next scale should be a portion scale going up to 16 oz (450 g); the third scale should be a baker table's scale to weigh flour and other dry products.

scoops Scoops are numbered according to the number of scoops contained in 32 oz (0.46 l). A #24 scoop for instance contains about 2¾ tbsp.

scraper Metal device to scrape dough together on the pastry table. It should be made of stainless steel. Some models are all metal, others have a wooden handle. Both work well.

sheet pan There can never be too many pans. Basically there are two types: plastic pans for cold storage and metal pans for baking. Sheet pans are available in many sizes, the standard size is 18 x 24 in. (450 x 600 mm). Metal pans should be made of aluminum. A catering operation needs full size and half size pans.

slicer Electric meat slicers are indispensable in catering operations. In many cases, the slicer is placed on a mobile stand, so it can be used in many parts of the kitchen, and is of convenient height. Very large operations find automatic slicers helpful.

spatula A number of types are available. The largest are the hamburger or sandwich turners, available solid or perforated. Both are needed. Narrow spatulas are needed to spread icing or cream on large surfaces. Butter spreaders are necessary to put small amounts of food in canape bases. Plastic spatulas, also called bowl knives, are handy to scrape out mixing bowls.

spoons Kitchen spoons are classified as perforated, slotted, and solid. The length of the handle varies. All three varieties are needed.

steamer Steamers have become an indispensable piece of equipment in restaurant kitchens. They are not essential in catering kitchens, but are practical to cook food quickly, and at the same time preserve nutrients. Small, table size electric steamers are self-contained and do not need a boiler.

steam table pans They should be made of stainless steel and are needed in many sizes. They are for holding hot and cold food and should not be used for roasting or baking food.

stoves Stoves' tops are classified as griddle tops; flat-tops with either a double ring or even-heat; and open burners.

Griddle tops are explained under *griddle*. Most stoves are available with split top combinations. Open burner tops are available in four and six burner units. For catering operations flat-top stoves are useful for boiling larger pots. Open burner stoves allow for smaller pots to be used.

Swiss braiser	Often called tilting frying pan. It is a useful piece of equipment, comparable to an electric skillet. The equipment is available in many sizes and in larger operations is practical to make fillings or saute food. The electric pan is more dependable than the gas-fired unit. The skillet should always be installed with a floor drain and a water outlet to make cleaning easy.
thermometers	Indispensable equipment for the conscientious operator. All refrigerators must be equipped with thermometers and all supervisory staff should carry food thermometers at all times.
whip, whisk	The name is interchangeable. Whips are classified as *roux* or *hard wire whips* and *piano wire whips*. Piano wire whips are also classified by shape: balloon whips are more rounded than straight whips. Roux or hard wire whips are used for stirring thick sauces; piano wire whips for beating lighter food, such as cream and egg whites. Balloon whips are used for beating egg whites. Both roux and piano wire whips are needed in a catering operation.
work tables	A catering operation can never have too many tables. The best tables are made of stainless steel and should be braised with under-shelves for added stability. Inexpensive tables will eventually sway and become unstable.
zester	Handy little tool to take off strips of peel from citrus fruits. It is not absolutely essential.

INDEX